# THE DIVIDED STATES OF AMERICA

*A Baby Boomer History Told Through 50 Years of Letters to the Editor*

## JOE EXUM, SR.

Exum, Joe Sr. *The Divided States of America: A Baby Boomer History Told Through 50 Years of Letters to the Editor*

Copyright © 2022 by Joe Exum, Sr.

ISBN: 979-8-218-04634-7

Library of Congress Catalog Number: 2022913999

# CONTENTS

# PREFACE

Political correctness has been defined as an opaque orthodoxy that teaches its disciples what to think rather than how to think, confusing coincidence with correlation and causes with symptoms in order to further hidden agendas using ends to justify the means. It is not clear when we began to accept judgment of Washington, Jefferson, Madison, and Monroe by those who have contributed nothing to art, medicine, or the sciences. Engaging philosophical bigots in dialogue to discover truth has left campuses void of the art of debate and left us intellectual zombies burdened with the most expensive educations in history.

This book is a collection of editorials which chronicle our history from Saul Alinsky's *Rules for Radicals* to the Clintons, to MoveOn.org, to Barack Obama. There are numerous reasons why this book may appeal to you. The author has listed the following Top reasons in hopes that you will buy the book:

- If you disdain political correctness and think that Californians are bizarre.

- If you are over the age of seventy, remember Ronald Reagan, and wonder why old white men are irrelevant.
- If you wonder what happened to the Party of Jefferson.
- If you vote AGAINST political candidates instead of FOR political candidates.
- If you think a college degree is overpriced and CEOs and academia are overpaid.
- If watching CNN is like scraping fingernails on a chalkboard.
- If you question whether kids too old to spank and too young to incarcerate are passing judgment on Washington, Lincoln, and Jefferson.
- If you wonder how much the free lunch costs.
- If you wonder if Silent Sam is keeping vigilance for maidenhood wherever he is.
- If you agree with Mark Twain: "There is no distinctly American criminal class…except Congress."
- If you wonder why no one retires to New Jersey from Alabama or South Korea to North Korea.
- If you wonder how to sustain a non-profit lemonade stand if you aren't George Soros.
- If you own a dog or cat.

# ABOUT THE AUTHOR

Joe Exum, Sr., the youngest son of Mary Wall and James G. Exum Sr., was born on April 8, 1943, in Snow Hill, North Carolina. He attended Snow Hill High School and graduated from Virginia Episcopal School in 1962, nicknamed *Crazy* by his classmates. He attended UNC-Chapel Hill and, upon graduation in 1966, married Sallie Jean Jackson of Rochester, New York, to whom he is still married.

He spent the next five years in Cheyenne, Wyoming, in the Strategic Air Command, where he was responsible for the safe operation of 10 ICBM Minuteman I missiles. Mr. Exum was honorably discharged as a captain in 1972 and he joined Happy Jack®, Inc., a business started by his father, where he began his political adolescence writing letters to the editor for the next fifty years. Mr. Exum attended the initial White House Conference on Small Business at the request of Senator Jesse Helms and was subsequently appointed to the N.C. Small Business Advocacy Council by Governor Jim Hunt. During that time Mr. Exum fostered three children—Jay, Manning, and Sallie—coached Little League baseball and youth basketball, and began two non-profit organizations: *Bogue Banks Environmental Stewardship Corporation* and *Friends of Man's Best Friend*.

In addition to sponsoring a Vietnamese Boat family, Mr. Exum has starred in the local womanless beauty pageant, the local "Dancing with the Stars," and performed as the omniscient "Great Swami." He has flown around the world, crossing the equator twice, traveled to all seven continents, swum in the Antarctic Ocean, and has raised over $3.5 million for various organizations. He has degrees in Political Science and Business Administration, and he holds two patents and numerous trademarks. He holds a NADA for Happy Jack® tapeworm tablets, is a duplicate bridge life master, an avid fly fisherman, inveterate golfer and an Eagle Scout!

# PROLOGUE

They call baby boomers "The Focus of Madison Avenue" because there are so many of us. Our parents belong to *the greatest generation* because they secured the blessings of liberty not only for us but also for the free world.

Now that life expectancy has become a reality, how will *baby boomers* be remembered? WOKES call us the "most selfish" generation, citing our unwillingness to pay tribute to a government too big to fail, that fails us miserably each day.

Our generation should be remembered as the *most prosperous*. In the firm belief that, "Personal freedom and economic freedom are inextricable," we are faced with the task of dividing plenty instead of scarcity.

> *"When men are left free by the state to engage in productive action, guided by self-interest above all, they do create the most efficient and powerful production system that is possible to their society. And what is the end result of these billions of individual decisions? It is the torrential outpouring of manmade wealth that characterizes the history of American capitalism—in which 28 percent of the total production of the*

*human race is created by only 5 percent of the world's population. American capitalism has generated the most astounding flood of imaginative goods and services ever to appear on the face of the earth. This is the system that has endowed the average American with the highest standard of living in the world and in history."*

—William Simon, Secretary of Treasury, *A Time for Truth*

We did not realize it at the time, but this ideal ended the Cold War without firing a shot: a conflict that had lasted for 37 years. It was this ideal that brought down the Berlin Wall and allowed us to be the "most prosperous" and arguably the most generous generation. This ideal contradicted every word of Mao Tse-Tung's *Little Red Book*, brought China from starvation to an economic juggernaut, and buried Karl Marx in the economic rubble of socialism or so we thought.

The essays in this book record a modern-day history of our generation in a series of "Letters to the Editor" beginning in 1976. Over the course of two generations, at least three hundred "Letters to the Editor" would be penned by Joe Exum, Sr., from Snow Hill, N.C., highlighting the struggle between individuals and institutions, and especially an overreaching government into small business. These essays have been published in the *Washington Post*, the *New York Times*, and the *Manchester Union Leader* among others as well as most daily newspapers in North Carolina.

At the beginning of most essays there is a brief description of the people or events related to the content of the essay.

This book is dedicated to my parents who incorporated Happy Jack® in 1946. The book is inspired by my career there, which began at the age of 11, and except for a five-year stretch in the Strategic Air Command, have been all my life. Everyone has a book in them, with your indulgence, this is mine.

# CHAPTER I

## RADICALIZED CANDIDATES, MOVEON.ORG, & SAUL ALINSKY

Martin Luther King, Jr., dreamed that someday we "would judge men by the content of their character and not the color of their skin." Ironically, Barack Obama did not fulfill that dream. His political success has been attributed to more people voting for him because he was black than people voting against him because he was black. Like *Seinfeld* character George Costanza's superficial pursuit of a black friend, Obama's election was superficial evidence that we had overcome racial prejudice in America. Barack Obama would embody *change we could believe in*. Unfortunately, Obama's experience, if not his character, left him woefully unqualified to be president. Removing Winston Churchill's bust from the Oval Office was a symbolic gesture portending a largely symbolic presidency that was devoted to diminishing the Reagan Revolution and the economic prosperity that collapsed the Berlin Wall, buried Marx in the economic history of socialism and ended the Cold War. The November 2016 cover of *Time* magazine described the Obama legacy best: *The Divided States of America*.

President Obama was truly an enigma when he burst onto the

political scene. Meteoric doesn't do justice to his political ascension to the presidency.

At the time, "liberal" and "socialist" were dirty political labels replaced with the new term, "progressive." Socialism was thought to have been buried by Reagan and the generation of prosperity he fostered by what the DNC/old media complex call "voodoo/trickle-down" economics. Who was this charismatic African-American who spoke of hopes and dreams you could believe and a fawning press choosing to believe he was not a disciple of MoveOn.Org, Saul Alinsky, Bill Ayers, and Jeremiah Wright?

Obama's political agenda was so radical, he could not get it passed in a Democratic Senate and Democratic House. Obamacare would be the culmination of what the Clintons began 12 years before. He opened the socialist closet by releasing a socialist genie that could not be returned to her bottle.

# HAPPY BIRTHDAY, DR. KING

*Justice Brett Kavanaugh was nominated to the Supreme Court in July 2018 by President Donald Trump and was confirmed as a Supreme Court Justice on October 6, 2018. Prior to being sworn in, allegations of sexual assault resulted in controversy surrounding Justice Kavanaugh's nomination. Justice Kavanaugh was questioned by the Senate Judiciary Committee from September 4th-7th, 2018. Both Justice Kavanaugh and Dr. Christine Blasey Ford, Ph.D., one of the women who accused Justice Kavanaugh of sexual assault, appeared in front of the Senate Judiciary Committee on September 27, 2018. Although the testimonies of Ms. Ford and others were discredited, Justice Kavanaugh continues to be harassed by extremists who opposed his nomination. The treatment of Justice Kavanaugh and his family is reminiscent of the television coverage of the Justice Thomas hearings which he described as a "high tech lynching."*

*Dr. Martin Luther King, Jr., faced much criticism in his time as a civil rights activist. The first federal Martin Luther King, Jr. Day occurred on January 20, 1986, In honor of Dr. King's birthday. Martin Luther King Jr. Day is held annually on the third Monday in January.*

Those who control the rhetoric, control the narrative. One editor's "insurrection" is another's "protest." Adapting rhetoric to vilify Kavanaugh and glorify Avenatti is classic. Dr. King was victim of just such propaganda. On Dr. King's national holiday…

———

## HAPPY BIRTHDAY, DR. KING

WHAT MARTIN LUTHER KING, JR. WAS, SENATOR, WAS A revolutionary. If revolutionary is synonymous with Communist in your book, then cancel Washington's and Lincoln's birthday!

Maybe "I have a dream!" doesn't sound like "Give me liberty or give me death!" Both were borne out of frustration, anger, and a longing for freedom. We are still experiencing Dr. King's revolution. God knows it hasn't been easy, but it has been without purge, oppression, or martial law. If that's Marxism, Senator, Joe Stalin's a humanitarian and Mother Theresa's a terrorist!

Thank you, Dr. King, and Happy Birthday!!!

October 5, 1983

# NEVER WASTE A CRISIS

*President Barack Obama was sworn into office on January 20, 2009. Much of his focus in his first few months in office was on economic recovery and reform as the U.S. was still in what some have termed "the Great Recession," which occurred from December 2007 to June 2009.*

*Jeremiah Alvesta Wright Jr. is a pastor emeritus of Trinity United Church of Christ in Chicago. Pastor Wright is best known for his anglophobic vitriol sermons and the influence it may have had and upon his most famous parishioner: Barack Obama. Following retirement, his beliefs and preaching were scrutinized when segments of his sermons about terrorist attacks on the United States and government dishonesty were publicized in connection with the 2008 presidential campaign of Barack Obama.*

---

## NEVER WASTE A CRISIS

PRESIDENT OBAMA'S INAUGURAL SPEECH WOULD HAVE BEEN MORE appropriate during the London Blitz. While Limbaugh rages and the New York Times raves, the problems we face now pale in comparison to 1980.

When President Obama was finishing high school, when Bill Ayers was designing pipe bombs, and when Jeremiah Wright was spewing racial vitriol, our nation was losing the Cold War. When first Lady Obama decried America, our diplomats were held hostage in Iran. Fear of hijacking gripped international travel and commerce. The economy struggled with double-digit unemployment, inflation, and interest rates. Social Security was bankrupt, and two decades of deficit spending threatened to rend the very fabric of our society. President Carter blamed the catastrophic conditions on America's malaise.

President-elect Reagan faced a hostile congress and a hostile press. And as if he didn't have enough problems, labor challenged the new president with an unprecedented illegal strike by air traffic controllers within days of taking his oath of office.

Invoking Washington's crossing the Delaware might have been more appropriate for Reagan's inaugural speech. On the contrary, Reagan was quite modest in calming our fears:

> *"The crisis we are facing today does not require of us the kind of sacrifice that ... so many thousands of others were called upon to make. It does require, however, our best effort, and our willingness to believe in ourselves and to believe in our capacity to perform great deeds; to believe that together, with God's help, we can and will resolve the problems which now confront us. And, after all, why shouldn't we believe that? We are Americans."*
> —Reagan's Inaugural Speech (1981)

February 3, 2009

# WHAT ABOUT BILL?

*William "Bill" Ayers founded Weather Underground in 1969 at the University of Michigan's Ann Arbor campus. Weather Underground was a far-left militant organization, which the FBI classified as a domestic terrorist group in 1970.*

*Members of Weather Underground, including Bill Ayers, planted several bombs in 1969 through the early 1970s. However, due to the FBI's use of illegal tactics throughout the investigation of Weather Underground, charges against Ayers were dropped.*

*Ayers later went on to teach at the University of Illinois. He retired as a professor in 2010. Although closely allied ideologically, politically, and geographically, both Obama and Ayers deny being in the same circle of friends.*

---

BILL AYERS IS LIVING THE AMERICAN DREAM. WHILE STRUGGLING AS a pipe bomb maker, Bill hit the lottery of higher education, receiving a $160,000,000 grant from a group of guilt-ridden, brain-dead, obscenely rich heirs to pay college professors to teach socialism and call it educational reform. Overnight, Bill went from social misfit to social engineer.

There's nothing unique or novel about Bill's philosophy: it's as old as Karl Marx. When the Berlin Wall came down, Bill's philosophy was buried in the communist squalor in East Berlin. His contempt for democracy and human rights are expressed by his resort to violence when he declares the debate to be over. If Bill had been around during the American Revolution, he would have fought for King George. If he had been in Tiananmen Square, he would have been driving the tank.

Regardless of how flawed free markets may be, the stubborn fact remains that we are faced with the problem of dividing abundance rather than scarcity at the end of the day. By learning *what* to think rather than *how* to think, students have been left with huge debts because of skyrocketing costs of college administrators and are ill-prepared to solve today's problems.

October 21, 2008

# THE CENTRAL PLANNERS

*President Barack Obama added to the national debt by $8.6 trillion or 74% according to the United States Treasury Department. In terms of dollars, this was the most the United States' debt has grown under a president at the time of writing; by percentage, the national debt grew by 74% (being the fifth most increase by percent, with the top percent increase occurring under President Franklin D. Roosevelt by 1048% fighting the Great Depression and World War II).*

---

*"Is life so dear, or peace so sweet, as to be purchased at the chains of slavery?"*
—Patrick Henry, Circa Boston Tea Party (1776)

PERHAPS THE MOST OUTRAGEOUS PROPAGANDA THE OBAMA DISCIPLES broadcast is the studied repudiation of the prosperity created by the Reagan marginal tax cuts in 1982. According to their propaganda, these cuts caused *massive deficits*. Not true. The tax cuts created unprecedented tax revenues and helped preserve Social

Security and Medicare. The *congress* caused unprecedented deficits by refusing to approve Reagan's budget and thus forcing a *continuing resolution* that allowed unbridled *spending* by the Democrat congress. In budgetary matters, *the president proposes; the Congress disposes*: Poli Sci 101.

The acceptance of the premise that *Reagan's marginal tax cuts caused massive deficits* is prerequisite to accepting the mind-numbing mantra: *the stimulus package has saved_millions of jobs (fill in the blank) and without it we would be in a great depression.* Wrong! Except for universities and government, the stimulus package has not only failed to create jobs but also, unlike the Reagan tax cuts, has been revenue *negative!*

Think about it. Sustainable jobs are not created by central planners regardless of IQ. Sustainable job creation is the spontaneous result of the natural economic law of market allocation of resources. Why didn't FDR create *Google*® instead of the CCC: the NFL instead of the IRS? *No Institution, no troika can have as much flair or creative intuition as an individual.* Obama and his messianic intellectuals have neither the vision nor the prescience to abrogate the natural law of economics any more than they can repeal the natural laws of physics!

What difference does it make?

As we spiral toward a national debt greater than our gross domestic product (GDP), increased regulations without cost/benefit analysis and increased government intervention in the marketplace, our grandchildren will become dependent upon central government for sustenance. Chronic unemployment, allocation of scarcity, and ultimately loss of personal liberty will become the fruits of *change you can believe in* and the legacy of Obama ideologues.

February 22, 2010

# THE OBAMA LEGACY

*From July 25-28, 2016, the Democratic National Convention was held in Philadelphia, Pennsylvania. There, with President Barack Obama's support, former Secretary of State Hillary Clinton received the presidential nomination.*

*In the 2016 presidential election, Clinton received an estimated 65,853,514 votes and 227 electoral votes, and Donald Trump received an estimated 62,984,82 votes and 304 electoral votes, winning him the election. Without the electoral and popular vote of New York and California, Senator Clinton would have received 113 electoral votes and ironically her popular vote would have exceeded that of her husband's 42% presidential victory. President Trump was sworn into office on January 20, 2017. Trump-haters, citing the electoral college as thwarting democracy, suffered a bitter defeat.*

---

*"...an abrasive agent to rub raw the resentments of the people of the community; to fan latent hostilities of many of the people to the point of overt expressions." Once such hostilities were "whipped up to a fighting*

*pitch," Alinsky continued, "the organizer steered his group toward confrontation, in the form of picketing, demonstrating, and general hell-raising. But at all times, the organizer's goal was not to lead his people anywhere, but to encourage them to take action on their own behalf."*

—*Rules for Radicals* by Saul Alinsky

Besides his considerable charisma and charm, Barack Obama will be remembered as the most successful community organizer since Saul Alinsky and the greatest threat to the Republic since the Great Depression. Unable to disguise his disdain for the Republic and the Constitution, his philosophical and cultural bigotry have left us the *Divided States of America*. Had such intolerance prevailed at the Constitutional Convention, we would be subjects of a Hamiltonian Imperial Presidency at best or the British Empire at worst.

The magnitude of the DNC/Hillary loss was masked by the popular vote in two states: New York and California. The defeat did not come at the hands of deplorables, racists, and cultural misfits. The DNC/news media complex was defeated by the Republic and the wisdom of the founding fathers.

The barbarians remain at the gate of liberty, and they will be relentless in their assault on the Trump administration. The stakes could not be higher; the fate of the American experiment hangs in the balance.

December 29, 2016

# SUCH MEN ARE DANGEROUS

*President Obama's inaugural address on January 20, 2009, covered a variety of topics, including the economic decline. The address also referenced Thomas Paine's* The American Crisis *with the quote, "Let it be told to the future world...that in the depth of winter, when nothing but hope and virtue could survive...that the city and the country, alarmed at one common danger, came forth to meet [it]." President Obama was the master of duplicity often quoting Reagan and Jefferson bringing "newspeak" to reality from George Orwell's* 1984.

---

THE GREEKS HAD MEASURED THE CIRCUMFERENCE AND DIAMETER OF the earth within 5 feet in 500 B.C., the Pythagorean theorem, and the circulatory system, all conformed to natural law and manifested eternal truths: *truths that last from generation to generation.* Perhaps the Gospel of John best describes Natural Law as: *"In the beginning was the Truth and the Truth was with God and the Truth was God."*

Homer introduced hubris interaction with natural law

governing human behavior when Odysseus exacts revenge in the *Odyssey*. Hubris connotes more than mere arrogance: hubris means *"becoming like the gods."* The ancient Greeks would view the 5-day weather forecast as hubristic.

In this light, the President's inaugural address was chilling. The president intends to control not only the economy but also the climate by placing himself squarely in conflict with natural law. Intoxicated with his political victory and enchanted with his myopic vision, Obama has truly ascended into a spiritual realm traditionally reserved for the saints. Trumpeted by his Marxist legions, he has ignored the lessons of ancient and modern Greece foreboding a legacy that history will surely record as Before Obama and After Obama.

January 23, 2013

# THE POWER OF APPOINTMENT

*In 2013, at the start of President Obama's second term, he nominated and appointed numerous individuals to join the administration. Nominees were appointed in a variety of posts, including within the State Department and Justice Department.*

*Also in 2013, it was found that the Internal Revenue Service (IRS) had subjected several political organizations that had requested tax-exempt status to what some felt was unjust and unnecessary levels of scrutiny. Conservatives felt that most organizations targeted were right-leaning, whereas liberals felt that right-leaning organizations weren't targeted specifically.*

*As a result, several investigations followed. The Justice Department announced in October 2015 that no criminal charges would be filed. Biden detractors point to Russia Collusion and January 6 political prisoners as further evidence of weaponizing the FBI and DOJ having made over 750 arrests for misdemeanor offenses in an FBI/DOJ dragnet relying on political informants while no arrests have been made for the June 2020 D.C. riots that required Secret Service vigil to avoid assassination concern.*

*"No Institution, no troika can have as much flair or creative intuition as an individual."*
    —*Author Unknown*

PERHAPS THE MOST IMPORTANT POWER OF THE PRESIDENCY IS THE power of appointment. Seemingly innocuous federal agencies become emboldened by invading privacy and wreaking emotional and economic havoc. In this light, Mr. Obama's denials of involvement in IRS, Justice Department, and State Department scandals ring hollow: the president is simply reaping what he has sown.

Mr. Obama is first and foremost an ideologue: he values institutions above individuals. He views the Constitution as an obstacle thwarting devotion to the state. *"You didn't build that"* devalues the individual's achievement and the unique genius it took *to build that.* The idea of *"spreading the wealth"* has historically ended with dividing scarcity, the demise of the middle class, and the violent overthrow of the institution responsible.

From organizations such as *MoveOn.org* and the *Environmental Liberation Front,* he has appointed those devoted to his neo-Marxist/Luddite agenda. Using deception and distortion to create crisis after crisis, his disciples have achieved unprecedented division and control over their subjects. Believing ends justify the means, the *Internal Revenue Service* has been enlisted to cast a pall over dissent.

Add the gruesome details of the Philadelphia abortion clinic and Jeremiah could not have trumpeted a confluence of scandal more withering than these. Pious invocation of the deity is unwarranted, however, a sober assessment of the selective morality justifying an agenda that is in such discord with natural law, the

Declaration of Independence and Constitution, is essential to the future of the great American experiment.

May 15, 2013

# RELENTLESS, RUTHLESS, AND AMORAL

*MoveOn.org was founded in September 1998 with the goal of advocating for progressive public policies and investing in the campaigns of demo- crat candidates. In the late 1990s, MoveOn.org became well-known for its email petitions. At the time, online petitions weren't as common as they are today, making the widespread impact of MoveOn.org unique at the time.*

*Originally MoveOn.org took its name from the Clinton/Lewinsky sexual scandals, imploring the government move on from the tawdry coverage to critical matters of state. Now called MoveOn, the organiza- tion continues to advocate for liberal policies, shares petitions via email campaigns, and helps raise funds for Democrat political candidates throughout the United States.*

*Before Twitter and Facebook, there was MoveOn.Org using email to generate staggering hordes of cash. The radical nature of MoveOn.Org cannot be overstated or the sophomoric propaganda it espouses. To achieve its radical agenda, it chose to support Obama over Hillary Clinton in the Democrat primaries. Using the power of appointment, Obama would spread the intractable tentacles of the deep state into the Department of State, the Department of Justice, the FBI, and the CIA.*

*Conspirators would argue the deep state fulfilled Obama's and his disciples' desires for a third term citing the XL Pipeline, signing the Paris Accord, ending the Stay in Mexico policy, exiting Afghanistan, renewing nuclear talks with Iran, and the Green New Deal. In defense of the conspirators, if it looks like a duck, quacks like a duck and walks like a duck, the existence of the deep state passes the "duck test."*

*William "Bill" Ayers is best known for founding a far-left militant organization known as Weather Underground in the late 1960s. This group committed acts of domestic terrorism throughout 1969 and 1970.*

*Saul Alinsky was a community organizer, left-wing activist, and author. Much of his work in Chicago, Illinois, was focused on encouraging poor populations to organize and take action. In the 1960s, some politicians accused Alinsky of having ties to communism, though Alinsky himself did not strictly identify as a communist. Alinsky and Dr. King were both active in the 1960s' Civil Rights movement and the FBI believed both were communists. Alinsky is probably best known for his book* Rules for Radicals *and his influence on Hillary Clinton while attending Yale.*

*Theodore "Ted" Kaczynski, also known as the Unabomber, is a domestic terrorist who mailed and delivered bombs to people's homes for nearly two decades (from the mid-1970s to the mid-1990s) before finally being caught in April 1996. As a result, three people died and almost two dozen individuals were injured.*

*Janet Kay Ruthven Hagan was an American lawyer, banking executive, and politician who served as a United States Senator from North Carolina from 2009 to 2015.*

*The Tea Party was founded in 2009 by fiscally conservative individuals with Newt Gingrich as their spokesman. It took its name from the Boston Tea Party in which the colonists threw English tea in Boston Harbor rather than pay British imposed taxes.*

MUCH HAS BEEN WRITTEN ABOUT THE INFLUENCE THAT THE TEA Party movement has had on national elections—most of it negative. Little is written about the Tea Party's murky nemesis, *MoveOn.Org,* that has had a dramatic impact on national elections, and if successful, the Great American Experiment will take a dramatic turn toward the idealism of Bill Ayers, Saul Alinsky, and Ted Kaczynski (the Unabomber).

Armed with degrees from University of California, Berkeley, Joan Blades and her husband sold their Silicon Valley startup during the Clinton dot com stock market bubble. With $13 million in proceeds, they began *MoveOn.Org* in 1998 to end the Clinton impeachment proceedings and *Move On* to more important affairs of government. MoveOn's decision to bank roll Barack instead of Hillary in the Democratic Primary of 2007 accelerated his meteoric rise to power and influence.

*MoveOn.org* has expanded to include a coalition of union labor, Occupy Wall Street, Monday Morning Moral Majority, New Bottom Line, Greenpeace, Rainforest Action Network, etc. Justin Ruben, Yale graduate and environmental activist, directs MoveOn from his home in Brooklyn, where he vows to end Republican control of the House once and for all.

To give some insight into MoveOn, in a recent email blast to their 8 million members, they chose to exploit the human suffering and devastation in the Philippines as an *opportunity* to move their global warming agenda through Congress. This group of Ivy League educated elitists is relentless, ruthless, well-funded, and amoral. They are intoxicated *with "more power than good women should want, or bad men should have."* Most important for North Carolinians, they will play an essential role in Kay Hagan's reelection success.

November 26, 2013

# HATE POLITICS

*In 1998, President Bill Clinton was investigated for having a sexual relationship with a 24-year-old White House intern, Monica Lewinsky.*

*President Clinton was impeached by the U.S. House of Representatives but was acquitted by the U.S. Senate. In civil court, however, he was fined and charged with contempt of court.*

*One of MoveOn.org's first viral email campaigns related to the impeachment of President Clinton, and the site became increasingly popular with liberal politicians and celebrities in the years to follow. Supporters of MoveOn.org have included Kathy Griffin.*

*In 2017, a man named John Hodgkinson shot five people, including several Republican congresspeople, at a baseball practice for the Republican baseball team in Alexandria, Virginia. Hodgkinson's social media presence showed that he held strong beliefs against the Republican party, which served as his motive for opening fire on the politicians.*

*Under occupation by Federal troops, the suspension of civil rights, and citizenship, the Ku Klux Klan (KKK) was founded in 1865 by Confederate veterans from the American Civil War in the aftermath of numerous lynchings of southern sympathizers and war veterans. Originally formed to protect their families against federal troop atrocities during Reconstruction, the KKK committed violent acts against Black people in the following decades, including murdering and lynching a multitude of black individuals.*

*In recent years, extremist groups such as KKK, BLM and Antifa have been linked to events such as the "Unite the Right" rally in Charlottesville, Virginia, in 2017.*

---

NOT HAVING SEX WITH MONICA LEWINSKY SPAWNED A PROPAGANDA machine the North Koreans wound envy. Born in Silicon Valley in 1998 during Clinton's impeachment, *MoveOn.Org* used social media to spread Anglophobic/Saul Alinsky vitriol and is often credited with the political success of Barack Obama and Bernie Sanders. Hollywood, Kathy Griffin, and the cast of Shakespeare in the Park would be disciples of this subversive cult.

John Hodgkinson was not playing Caesar in his violent effort to kill Republican Congressmen even though radicalized Democrats suggested Scalise got what he deserved. The Democrat Party has distanced itself from the KKK over the past 50 years: it is time the DNC distanced itself from the political intolerance and bigotry espoused at *MoveOn.Org*.

June 28, 2017

# RADICALIZED PRESIDENTIAL CANDIDATES

*As President Barack Obama's second term neared its end in 2015, Secretary of State Hillary Clinton and Senator Bernie Sanders were both vying for the Democratic National Convention's nomination for president. Within the Democratic party, supports of Senator Sanders were concerned about potential bias from the DNC against Senator Sanders. Ultimately, Clinton was chosen as the Democratic National Convention's presidential nominee on July 26, 2016.*

---

**Question**: "What do Barack Obama, Bernie Sanders, and Hillary Clinton have in common?"

**Answer**: Ted Kaczynski, Saul Alinsky, Fidel Castro, Bill Ayers, Chicago, Community Organization, Harvard, Yale, *MoveOn.Org.*

WHEN MOST OF US WERE STUDYING PLATO, ARISTOTLE, AND THOMAS Jefferson, Hillary Clinton was seeking direction from Saul Alinsky having become disenchanted with the American experiment. Saul viewed America as "haves and have nots" vowing to radicalize the "have nots" to overthrow the "haves." Among Barack Obama's inner circle of friends was Bill Ayers who escaped incarceration for acts of terror as founder of Weather Underground. Bernie Sanders openly embraced Fidel Castro's success in establishing a brutal communist dictatorship 90 miles from Miami. Known as the Unabomber for his acts of terror, Ted Kaczynski is often credited for being the father of *Environmentalism*, viewing technology as the enemy of society. Nothing distinguishes *Move-On.Org* from the psychotic anarchists of the 1970s except their ability to raise money for Barack Obama and Bernie Sanders.

To accept the solutions offered by radicalized candidates is to ignore history. Why has no one escaped Miami to Cuba? From South Korea to North Korea? Why was no one shot while climbing the wall to East Berlin? The radical policies of this administration have not only divided us but also destabilized our political process. This was the goal of Alinsky, Kaczynski, and Ayers, and, the accomplishment of Fidel Castro.

> *"The crisis we are facing today does not require of us the kind of sacrifice that… so many thousands of others were called upon to make. It does require, however, our best effort, and our willingness to believe in ourselves and to believe in our capacity to perform great deeds; to believe that together, with God's help, we can and will resolve the problems which now confront us. And, after all, why shouldn't we believe that? We are Americans."*

—Reagan's first inaugural address.

April 11, 2016

# CHAPTER II

## NEO-ABOLITIONISM/NEO-CIVIL RIGHTS/ CULTURAL CLEANSING

*Michael Avenatti is an infamous attorney who has pleaded guilty of embezzling millions of dollars from his clients. Most recently, he was sentenced to four years in prison for stealing approximately $300,000 from his client, Stormy Daniels. Avenatti would negotiate settlements for his clients and then lie to them about the terms of their settlements in order to deposit funds into his own trust accounts. Mr. Avenatti considered running against President Trump in the 2020 presidential election and was endorsed by CNN.*

---

## HATE POLITICS

The politics of division have not overlooked cultural values that are largely divided along the Mason-Dixon Line. Those who get their history from social media and their news from CNN, not only get fake news but fake history. Watching CNN embrace Avenatti as a possible presidential candidate would be comical if it were not so irresponsible making one wonder why the FCC does not unplug CNN.

June 2017

# WHAT IT WAS, WAS
# HAM-IL-TON

*The musical,* Hamilton, *by Lin Manuel Miranda, is about one of our nation's foremost founding fathers, Alexander Hamilton. Based on Ron Chernow's book* Alexander Hamilton, *it has many highs and lows from Hamilton's early years to making his way to the American Colonies.*

*"The Andy Griffith Show" is a television show about a widowed sheriff of Mayberry, North Carolina. He and his son, Opie, live with Andy's Aunt Bee. Because there is almost no crime in Mayberry, Andy spent most of his time philosophizing and calming down his cousin, Deputy Barney Fife. Upon graduation from UNC, "What It Was, Was Football" launched the North Carolinian on an unprecedented recording, television, and Broadway career.*

*"Amos 'n' Andy" was a sitcom that aired on television from 1951-1953. It featured two African-American actors, Alvin Childress and Spencer Williams, Jr. The stories primarily centered around The Kingfish's schemes to get rich by trying to dupe his brothers in the Mystic Knights of the Sea Lodge. The actor who played Amos was actually white.*

*Mr. Bojangles is Bill "Bojangles" Robinson. He was a famous early 20th century African-American dancer who is best known for dancing roles with Shirley Temple in films of the 1930s. Bill, the first black tap dancer to break through the Broadway color line and became one of the highest paid performers of his day.*

*N.C. Baby Boomers grew up with the characters in this essay and can probably answer the trivia question:*

*What was the flip side of "What it Was, Was Football"? You guessed it: Romeo & Juliet.*

———

Do you remember Andy Griffith's "What it Was, Was Football"? Griffith's description of his first football game was hilarious, and so was DCAP's version of the Broadway play "Hamilton," especially if you could overlook the celebration of New York's Hamilton at the expense of Virginia's Jefferson.

Regardless, the comedy begins with Alexander Hamilton seeking fortune, sacred honor, and a good life when he gets wind of Virginians offering lives, fortunes, and sacred honor. He lands in New York where farmers are making a wartime fortune by selling their crops to feed the British army. Hamilton becomes the *Father of Inside Trading* hoarding worthless treasury notes by using the ingenious creation of a bank that could lend money to itself to redeem the worthless notes.

Enter the villain, Thomas Jefferson. Cast as a cross between Amos and Andy's Kingfish when he grins and Mr. Bojangles when he dances, the hilarity does not end here. George Washington is cast as a diminutive Danny DeVito, Aaron Burr as a power forward, and James Madison lost on stage and history.

Relying upon Chernow's imagination, Hamilton becomes a war hero and vocal abolitionist, and Jefferson becomes a draft-dodging slave owner vacationing in France during the war. Then tragedy strikes just when things seemed headed for a happy hereafter. Not wishing to miss his shot, Hamilton, well, gets shot. (Does that make sense?)

In summary, the play has the shock value of "Jesus Christ Superstar" and the historical creativity that Disney studios would envy, confirming the Greatest Showman's belief, "No one ever went broke underestimating the taste of the American public!"

November 15, 2018

# RICHMOND FALLS TO WOKE YANKEES

*A variety of Confederate monuments that were built in Richmond in the late 1800s were removed from Richmond's Monument Avenue in 2020. One of the most well-known statues was the Robert E. Lee Monument, which was built in 1890.*

*In January 2022, it was tentatively announced that the Robert E. Lee Monument would be placed in the Black History Museum and Cultural Center of Virginia. After his citizenship was stripped by Congress in 1865 and the Custis plantation was confiscated to become Arlington Cemetery, General Lee would have his citizenship restored in 1972. The treatment of General Lee is troubling lending credence to charges of cultural cleansing.*

*Ronald Chernow, an American writer, journalist and biographer, has written bestselling historical non-fiction biographies, including* Alexander Hamilton. *Chernow once described Southerners as having "ingratiating manners." The financial success of the Broadway play changed the publish or perish dynamic to publish and prosper using poetic license with history, religion, and the liberal arts.*

AFTER 150 YEARS OF SIEGE, RICHMOND HAS BEEN TAKEN: damnyankee WOKES tore down General Lee's statue, a la Saddam Hussein. Not to be outdone by NYT Project 1619, the Atlantic magazine characterized General Lee as a slave owning white supremacist, traitor to the Union, and responsible for thousands of deaths to protect ownership of slaves. This fake history makes Chernow's *Hamilton* look historically respectable.

How so?

Lee was not a secessionist. He did not want war against his West Point classmates or his brothers from the Mexican wars.

When Lincoln sent troops into his beloved state of Virginia, Lee was faced with disloyalty to his state or to the union. He chose the latter.

In what Lee described as a colossal failure in leadership, both North and South, Lincoln's invasion of the South was a devastating miscalculation the South could be vanquished in a short period of time.

Since Lee was never elected to any office, the death of 800,000 Americans should more appropriately be attributed to Lincoln and Davis.

The war was not about white supremacy. The war was fought for Southern independence for much the same reasons outlined in the Declaration of Independence 90 years previously.

Southern slavery was the precipitating issue but did not account for the length of the war. Fear of Northern reprisal in what became known as "The Southern Cause" prolonged the war. 12 years of Southern occupation by federal troops to cleanse the Southern culture justified those fears.

General Lee did not own slaves: the Custis family owned slaves. After the war, Arlington was taken from the Custis family as well as Lee's citizenship.

General Lee enjoyed mythical statue not only in the South as de facto spokesman but also internationally for his battlefield victories against overwhelming odds. He was the Southern icon for Southern culture. It was Lee's belief victory at Gettysburg might have brought an early peace. In fact, it was a tactical and strategic blunder. Removing his statue will do nothing to diminish his image.

Jefferson was prophetic when he described slavery as an existential threat to the Union in 1793. Embracing the resilience of Southerners, especially their women and children, through the terror of Reconstruction is not to ignore the institution of slavery but to give slavery its proper place in history. In the final analysis, we are the nation of Washington, Jefferson, Madison, & Monroe, regardless of events in Richmond.

September 12, 2021

# REPARATIONS

*In June 2022, California unveiled the first slave reparations report in the United States. Some of the recommendations for these reparations included prison reform, facilitated access to mortgages, and free tuition to state universities. The report outlined harms suffered by descendants of enslaved people long after slavery was abolished. President Joe Biden met with black U.S. legislators to express his support for a study on how the United States could compensate the descendants of black slaves which raises numerous questions. For example, among Thomas Jefferson's descendants, who would pay whom? Should the ancestors of those who died at Gettysburg be exempt? Normandy? Were the blessings of liberty secured with the Emancipation Proclamation?*

---

DO YOU FEEL GUILTY BECAUSE DESCENDANTS OF SOUTHERN SLAVERY have not received reparation payments? If so, it's probably because Ivy League New Yorkers with a Bronx/Brooklyn perspective on the universe are busy rewriting history novels about the era of Southern *Reconstruction* authorizing Southern *Destruction* in hopes of colonizing the South. According to their redactions, descendants of Jefferson, Washington, and Lee should foot the bill as well as have their names erased from history.

Not so fast, carpetbaggers!

First, "white supremacy" did not begin with Southern slavery. Racial supremacy has been around for as long as ethnocentrism. White supremacy was used to justify British colonialism. The British believed that they were God's emissaries, and their subjects were the "White man's burden." The British were as arrogant as they were brutal: the colonies, both free and slave, experienced the hob nailed boot of British occupation.

Okay, Professor, who should pay?

There are two sides to this history. Relying upon Dray and Drummond, Southerners should be reimbursed by northern textile merchants who confiscated their land under martial law during Reconstruction. The "Freedmen" argued they had worked the land, therefore it belonged to them. Cloaked in self-righteousness and backed by Federal troops, carpet-baggers exploited the South like a California gold rush. Freedmen were expected to sign indentured contracts and go back to work in the cotton fields. Naively, Freedmen believed that they were "free" and refused to sign "labor contracts." Like indentured servants, they were beaten into submission by their new masters.

Finding moral high ground in the Reconstruction era is a difficult task at best. Perhaps academia has profited most by exonerating merciless economic predators posing as abolitionists!

April 30, 2019

# NEO-ABOLITIONISM

*There has been a push in the United States to remove the Confederate flag from buildings, NASCAR, books, etc. Many people feel that the flag is a symbol of racism, slavery, and division. It all depends* on those offended. *However, the flag that we see as representing the Confederacy was only one of many flags flown in the South during the Civil War. It is the Confederate battle flag.*

*The Washington D.C. National Football League (NFL) team abandoned the name Redskins in July 2020. The name that had been the team's mascot dating back to 1937. Some say that the name had long been deemed offensive and was routinely denounced by Native American groups as an ethnic slur. Please be tolerant of Baby Boomers who still pull for the Redskins and Sonny Jurgensen.*

---

*"The evil men do lives after them. The good is oft interred with their bones."*
—Julius Caesar

WHAT BEGAN WITH THE REMOVAL OF TOM SAWYER FROM PUBLIC libraries and the Confederate Flag from state capitals has escalated into the wholesale destruction of memorials to George Washington, Thomas Jefferson, Charles Aycock, Robert E. Lee, and now the destruction of Silent Sam. These actions were justified in the name of racial harmony citing the institution of slavery that was sowing seeds of white supremacy and racism that linger today.

A common thread runs through these recriminations—all have roots in the South. The inference that racism is somehow a legacy of the South is as offensive as it is misleading. The neo-abolitionist notion that a cultural cleansing will end the scourge of racism is pure bigotry stoked by Hollywood, Broadway, and revisionist history. This sanctimonious belief is a classic example of *spotting the splinter in our neighbor's eye*. The race riots of the sixties are generational reminders that racism has no geographical or cultural boundary.

Regardless of what we saw at the Super Bowl, the pursuit of social justice did not originate with the National Football League. Achieving social justice is as old as Socrates. Stoking bigotry fills church coffers and ballot boxes far more efficiently than stoking tolerance. It is the milk of division politics, thematic for *MoveOn.org*, and essential for a Divided States of America. We have truly "…met the enemy, and he is us."

February 20, 2019

# THE CITY OF WOKES

*On February 22, 2022, the Raleigh News & Observer interviewed Chris Suggs, the youngest Kinston City Council member and founder of the nonprofit Kinston Teens. In the featured article, Suggs talked about problems impacting youth in his community.*

THE RALEIGH *NEWS & OBSERVER'S* HATCHET JOB ON LIFE EAST OF I-95 is a classic case of spotting the "splinter in your neighbor's eye" while ignoring the "log in your own" seen through a woke prism. Forsaking Jesse Helms' roots, RDU has embraced Carpetbaggers who moved to Raleigh-Durham and transformed the City of Oaks to the City of Wokes; most of whom have never been east of I-95.

The problem with RDU, besides publishing the N&O and Duke, is they are too far from the Atlantic Ocean. So when it gets too hot in the summer, protestors torch downtown. RDU has a lot more problems. For example, there are only 5 seasons in Raleigh: Traffic Jam which lasts for 12 months and the others. In Kinston we have 8 seasons including duck, turkey, rabbit, and deer. Wokes rely on CNN and the NYT for <u>what</u> to think that day. Kinstonians rely upon the King James Bible on <u>how</u> to think for the rest of their lives.

You may not be old enough to remember the Stanley Cup. It's not exactly clear who Stanley was, but the Charlotte Observer made it clear, he had no connection to the Wide, Wide World of Wrestling or the considerable prestige the WWW brought to the Woke-infested State of Charlotte. Prestige is very important for the images of Charlottetonians and RDU'ans alike. If Jesse were alive today, he might suggest making a Wildlife Preserve out of the Triangle leading the nation in carbon neutrality while adopting the motto: "To Seem Rather than to Be!"

Lifestyles have no dollar signs and without dollar signs, statistics are problematic. Regardless, in the final analysis, the N&O article exudes envy of a lifestyle more priceless than expensive.

(The N.C. State Motto is "To Be Rather than to Seem.")

May 3, 2022

# IN DEFENSE OF SAM

*At the University of North Carolina at Chapel Hill (UNC), the Confederate Monument commonly known as "Silent Sam," is a bronze statue of a Confederate soldier by Canadian sculptor, John A. Wilson. The statue stood on McCorkle Place at the university from 1913 until it was pulled down by protesters in 2018. The statue's base was removed in 2019. Over the years, hundreds have gathered on the university's campus to share their views on "Silent Sam" which has been one of controversy and animosity. Sam was an icon to women's virtue in the 60s, standing vigil and firing a shot each time a UNC virgin passed. Co-eds were not so easily offended by Sam's silence at their passing and were not responsible for his removal.*

As the oldest state-supported university, the University of North Carolina occupied a unique place in our country's history. As UNC adopts a WOKE academic culture marked by anglo-phobic, afro-centric ideological bigotry, UNC's legacy should be remembered in terms of Before Silent Sam and After Silent Sam and hope the historical prestige generated before Silent Sam will distinguish it from today's overpriced diplomas taught by overpaid academic zombies too old to spank and too young to incarcerate.

---

RECENTLY, ORANGE COUNTY DISTRICT JUDGE SCARLETT COMPARED Silent Sam to Hitler, and, by extension, the human suffering of slaves to that of the Holocaust. Based upon her remarks, it is not clear how well Ms. Scarlett knew Sam or Adolph Hitler.

Statistically speaking, Sam had not celebrated his twenty-first birthday when he enlisted, choosing loyalty to his home state over loyalty to the Union. He was one among 4,000 from the University; some fought for the North, most fought for the South. Even though he grew up in an agrarian setting, he probably didn't own slaves even though he defended a culture that depended upon slavery unlike his counterpart in Blue who defended a culture that depended upon indentured servitude. Sam never ran for office. He would never celebrate his twenty-fifth birthday. Sam's mother would endure the loss of her son and twelve years of Reconstruction atrocities.

Ironically, using mobs that obliterate history in order to rewrite history is not only a hallmark of Hitler but that of every tyrant since the Exodus that would enslave their subjects. Judge Scarlett views history through the prism of neo-abolitionism and the fury it stokes. Nonetheless, as offensive as her remarks may have been, they were equally as chilling. God forbid Sam or his legacy ever appear in her courtroom.

September 2020

# CULTURAL CLEANSING

*In 2013, a Black-centered political movement was created called Black Lives Matter. It began with a social media hashtag, #BlackLivesMatter, after the acquittal of George Zimmerman in the shooting death of Trayvon Martin back in 2012. Black Lives Matter (BLM) appears to stand for life, liberty, and the pursuit of happiness especially for wronged African Americans. Their appearance is deceiving, relying on accusations of systemic racism and ignoring systemic drug addiction. One of the leaders stated in a 2015 interview that they are trained organizers and Marxists.*

*The organization has been known to foster the ideas of replacing the Western nuclear family with the state and defunding the police while misappropriating millions in donations. As the deaths of young blacks escalate, BLM detractors have renamed the seditious organization Some Black Lives Matter void of virtue or purpose.*

---

IT'S BEEN A ROUGH MONTH IF YOU'RE AN OLD WHITE MAN FROM THE South. The rhetorical lash of racism has been unrelenting, pouring verbal brine into wounds opened during Southern Reconstruction. Caught in the crossfire between professional politicians and professional racists, "news organizations" continue cleansing Southern Culture with a fervor Goebbels and Chernow would be proud.

Noticeably, most of the violence took place in New York, Detroit, Minnesota, Baltimore and New Jersey. Perhaps a Northern Cultural cleansing would end the stench of racism but there's not much Northern Culture to cleanse: no Washingtons, Jeffersons, Madisons, or Monroes. Okay. Rocky Balboa and a dubious Pocahontas. No flag or Tom Sawyers. No "ingratiating manners."

There is Wall Street: the mother of income inequality and the privileged Ivy Leaguer class. No reparations for ancestors of indentured servitude because most died chained to the machines that generated millions for the obscenely rich robber baron class. Otherwise, there's just not much Northern Culture to cleanse.

Cleansing cultures will only serve Saul Alinsky's *Rules for Radicals* in destabilizing the representative Republic founded to unite divisive cultures. Cultural divisiveness will not end until professional racists and professional politicians have squeezed every vote and every dollar from the rhetoric generated in the elusive pursuit of social justice.

June 12, 2020

# IN PRAISE OF OLD WHITE MEN

*President Donald Trump nominated Brett Kavanaugh as associate justice of the Supreme Court of the United States on July 9, 2018, to succeed retiring justice Anthony Kennedy.*

*Several days after the Senate Judiciary Committee hearings regarding his nomination, it was reported psychology professor Christine Blasey Ford had written a letter to Senator Dianne Feinstein in July accusing Kavanaugh of sexual assault while they were both in high school in 1982. The Committee postponed its vote and invited both Kavanaugh and Blasey Ford to a public Senate hearing. Additionally, two other women, Deborah Ramirez and Julie Swetnick, also accused Kavanaugh of separate past instances of sexual assault.*

*On October 2018, following an FBI investigation into the allegations, Brett Kavanaugh was confirmed to the Supreme Court by a Senate vote of 50-48. Although the accusations by partisan accusers were discredited, Justice Kavanaugh and his family continue to be threatened by extremists. Similarly, Justice Thomas characterized television coverage of his congressional hearing as a "high tech lynching."*

*Kermit the Frog is a Muppet character created and originally performed by Jim Henson. Serving as the everyman protagonist of numerous Muppet productions, Kermit performed the hit single, "Bein' Green."*

---

IF KERMIT THE FROG THINKS BEING GREEN IS TOUGH, HE OUGHT TO try hopping in the shoes of old white men. *Progressive-liberal* misandrists want to suspend civil rights, so crazy white women can level charges of sexual assault with reckless disregard for due process. Apparently, there is no statute of limitation for old, straight, white male libido. (Thomas Jefferson case in point.)

Misandrists' disdain aside, old white men's lives matter. Watching grandchildren cry at the loss of a grandfather substantiate this belief. With total disregard for the wife and daughters of Judge Kavanaugh, Democrats have definitively answered the question "Have you no decency Senator McCarthy?" with a resounding "Yes, we have no decency!"

September 21, 2018

# DUE PROCESS BE DAMNED

On January 7, 2018, the 75<sup>th</sup> Golden Globes award ceremony was held in Beverly Hills, California. During the event produced by Dick Clark Productions in association with the Hollywood Foreign Press Association, talk show host and celebrity Oprah Winfrey received the Cecil B. DeMille Lifetime Achievement Award. During her acceptance speech, Ms. Winfrey spoke about many topics including harassment and assault.

In 2006, three Duke University lacrosse players were charged with first-degree forcible rape, sexual offense, and kidnapping after a female stripper accused them of raping her while she performed at one of their parties.

Duke spent $100M in legal fees, settling with the defendants for $60M. Mike Nifong, the D.A. who orchestrated the conspiracy, was disbarred. The woman killed her boyfriend and was sentenced to 14-18 years in jail.

_"Rescue us from becoming the evil that happened to us."_
—Steve Daugherty

MANY HAVE HAILED OPRAH WINFREY'S SPEECH AT HOLLYWOOD'S latest self-adulation ceremony as presidential. Praising women who have come forward to accuse their male oppressors, Oprah envisioned a "new horizon" for women. The crowd was mob like in their response echoing the sentiment basic civil rights should be suspended to encourage women to come forward. For the audience, the speech was wildly inspirational: for a grandfather of grandsons, the message was bone chilling.

One does not have to be an expert in Freudian psychology to posit for every woman hater there is probably a man hater. Has Hollywood forgotten the injustice perpetrated in the name of political correctness at Duke University? Without due process exposing corruption from accused to prosecutor, 3 grandsons would be serving their 10th year of a 30-year sentence.

The Obama administration's disdain for the rule of law and willingness to suspend civil rights to accommodate extreme agendas is now a matter of history. Reversing Obama-era policies on campus sexual assault under Title IX by the Secretary of Education is not only another repudiation of the Obama administration but also a relief to grandfathers and grandmothers with grandsons and granddaughters.

January 10, 2018

# NEO-ABOLITIONISM

*The confederate statue commonly known as "Silent Sam" was toppled down by protesters in August 2018. This statue dominated the main entrance of the University of North Carolina at Chapel Hill for over a century. One day after classes started in August of 2018, the Confederate Statue called Silent Sam was toppled by a mob of students and teachers, in an internet inspired fever pitch of animosity toward Sam. Later, in 2019, the campus chancellor Carol Folt had the pedestal and any other remnants removed from the university's grounds.*

---

IF YOU WERE WATCHING THE HISTORY CHANNEL LAST WEEK, THE events in Chapel Hill looked eerily like the events used to bring Lenin, Stalin, and Hitler to power. Reminiscent of the KKK, law enforcement and the Chancellor appear intimidated by the drunken mob that tumbled the Civil War memorial erected in 1913 by granddaughters of loved ones lost on both sides of that war, apparently because neo-abolitionists were offended by its presence.

The "Blessings of Liberty" have come at great cost, not only at Gettysburg but also at Normandy. The carnage on the Southside of Chicago serves as a reminder the "Blessings of Liberty" have not been secured for everyone. For those offended by the destruction of this memorial, "Shutting out the light to expose the shadows" only serves those who celebrate "The Divided States of America."

August 24, 2018

# NEO-CIVIL RIGHTS

*In 2016, civil rights leader Reverend Al Sharpton and his organization held a protest in a strip mall just yards away from Dolby Theater where the Oscars were being held. Sharpton stated at the protest that it would be the last night of an all-white Oscar awards. After speaking, he led the protesters in a parking lot march, chanting, "Green-light diversity" and "Diversify the Academy". The Academy had promised Sharpton and his organization, National Action Network (NAN), that they would change by not only nominating people of color but also allowing them to be in the decision-making process. While these actions are to be acknowledged, they pale in comparison to the social justice advances achieved by Baby Boomers. In retrospect, we should be embarrassed at just how far we had to come.*

---

FIFTY-THREE YEARS AGO ON A TRIP TO ROCHESTER, NEW YORK, TO meet my future in-laws, civil rights protestors burned Joseph Avenue to the ground. Today, my son is in Charlotte on business. Naturally, I am concerned for his safety.

If we believe Rev. Al Sharpton and the BLM movement, affirmative action, school integration, and the Civil Rights Act of 1963 have done little to relieve hostilities. Listening to Sharpton's flock call their oppressors "white devils" is an echo of the Nation of Islam movement that captured Muhammad Ali's devotion in 1965. Oppression was palpable in 1965. In 2016, oppression is not as transparent.

Blaming "white devils" and the institution of slavery ignores the real and present danger of the heroin/meth epidemic that has spawned gang violence and instilled fear in black and white citizens alike. For those gripped with fear, law enforcement is expected to keep us safe from the psychotic behavior of addicts and the vultures that thrive on their addiction.

Where this epidemic is rampant, hope is dead. How do we renew hope? Economics is a dismal science. Nonetheless, assuming there is a correlation between hope and prosperity, economic policy that fosters vigorous growth in the private sector is essential for domestic and international stability. In the 1980s the media called such policy Voodoo Economics. Today we call it "The Reagan Revolution."

September 22, 2016

# BRING BACK SPEAKER BAN

*Professor Mike Dyson gave a highly criticized commencement speech at the University of North Carolina at Chapel Hill in 1996. Dyson's use of occasional profanity, criticism of Michael Jordan, and the overall challenging tone of the speech regarding the American dream were found to be controversial. Some students and parents walked out during the speech. Several parents and alumni wrote to Chancellor Michael Hooker with complaints.*

*On June 26, 1963, the North Carolina General Assembly passed the Act to Regulate Visiting Speakers, later known as the Speaker Ban Law. The law forbade anyone to speak on a University of North Carolina campus who was a known member of the Communist Party, or who was known to advocate overthrow of the United States Constitution, or who had invoked the Fifth Amendment in respect of communist or "subversive" connections.*

*During the McCarthy hearings, McCarthy always led his questioning with, "Are you now, or have you ever been a Communist?" followed by, "Do you know or have you ever been associated with members of the Communist party?" Based upon Condoleezza Rice's campus experience and the January 6 congressional inquisition, ques-*

*tioning would begin, "Did you vote for Donald Trump? If not, are you now a Republican or have you ever been a Republican?" Regardless of party affiliation, the dearth of critical thinking among academia is not unique to UNC.*

———

THE PROBLEM WITH MIKE DYSON'S COMMENCEMENT SPEECH AT UNC was not the language he used. (Although he would have been court martialed as a drill sergeant.) The problem with Mike Dyson's commencement speech was that his message was trite. The philosophy of social victimization is kept alive by limousine liberals to keep democrats in power and Afro-Americans in political bondage.

If Mr. Dyson truly believes that Afro-Americans must depend upon "the kindnesses of strangers" to achieve the American Dream, I suggest he read *The Skin Game* and *Content of Our Character*. And if Mr. Dyson is the University's idea of "intellectual stimulation," I suggest Chancellor Hooker bring back keg parties and book some old-timey communist speakers from Speaker Ban days.

December 18, 1996

# ACADEMIC PROSTITUTES

*Patrick Albert Moore is a Canadian industry consultant, the past president of Greenpeace Canada, and a former activist. He is known for his criticism of the environmental movement abandoning science and logic for emotion, scare tactics, disinformation, and sensationalism.*

*Orrin H. Pilkey is an American Professor Emeritus of Earth and Ocean Sciences, Nicholas School of the Environment, at Duke University, and founder and director emeritus of the Program for the Study of Developed Shorelines (PSDS), currently based at Western Carolina University. Orrin is best known for the North Carolina Coastal Area Management Act and his war on Rich Oceanfront Property Owners (ROPO). "Retreat from the shoreline" became his mantra in hopes of fulfilling his lifelong ambition of making coastal beaches state parks.*

*William Francis Sutton, Jr. was an American bank robber. For his talent at executing robberies in disguises, he gained two nicknames, "Willie the Actor" and "Slick Willie."*

RECENTLY, PATRICK MOORE, COFOUNDER OF GREEN PEACE, distanced himself from the Intergovernmental Panel on Climate Change (IPCC) expressing concern that the environmental movement begun in the 1970s has been hijacked by political activists who cloak their capricious social agendas with crippling demands on the private sector to prevent environmental apocalypse. Unfortunately, the Governor's Scientific Panel on Coastal Energy looks just like the 1999 Scientific Panel on Coastal Hazards—colleagues and coauthors of Orrin Pilkey espousing Orrin's radical science in his private warfare on coastal development.

Billed as the best minds in North Carolina by the Governor's office, the panel is composed primarily of academic prostitutes who would declare the world flat if they thought there was grant money available. Predictably, in the case of coastal energy alternatives, the panel will recommend wind turbines in lieu of developing natural gas deposits. If the panel were as honest as Willie Sutton, they would answer, "'Cause that's where the money is," when asked why! Wind turbines make no economic, environmental, or scientific sense especially in light of the nuclear accident in Japan.

Our country has not divided scarcity since the 1930s. With varying degrees of severity, we are seeing the tip of the iceberg of scarcity from Cairo, Egypt, to Madison, Wisconsin. In a state already living far beyond its means, we can no longer afford the luxury of bad policy decisions to satisfy reckless demands of radical social engineers who cloak their agendas in the invidious orthodoxy of political correctness.

March 22, 2011

# AFRO-CENTRISM AND
# PRESIDENT'S DAY

*President's Day was first established in 1885 to honor George Washington's birthday, February 22. It became a U.S. federal holiday in 1971 and is currently celebrated on the third Monday of every February to honor the combined birthdays of George Washington and Abraham Lincoln.*

*Also, every February the United States honors the sacrifices and contributions of African Americans who helped shape our nation by celebrating Black History Month. The month of February was chosen because it coincides with the birthday of Abraham Lincoln (February 12) and Frederick Douglass' birthday (February 14). Black History Month began in 1926 as Negro History Week.*

IF THE TREND TOWARD AFRO-CENTRISM CONTINUES, THIS COULD BE the last Black History Month in which we celebrate Washington's and Jefferson's presidency. Expunging William Saunders and William Aycock from history and the campuses they inspired because they were members of the KKK leaves Washington and Jefferson in a precarious position as slaveholders.

Ironically, the civil rights movement in this country did not begin with the Black Panthers or the NAACP. In fact, the KKK was begun to restore civil rights when Federal Troops occupied the South and suspended all civil rights during Reconstruction. Before that, Boston Harbor provided the crucible, which became the greatest civil rights movement since the Magna Carta.

Expunging Reconstruction from history and vilifying great leaders as slave owners amounts to little more than "book burning." Book burnings have been essential for every fanatical agenda to succeed, whether communism, Nazism, Environmentalism, or Afro-Centrism. Taking the names down is easy. Removing the buildings that they inspired and the civil rights that they secured would give us all a better understanding of why we celebrate Black History Month and President's Day.

March 2011

# CHAPTER III

## INDIVIDUALS & INSTITUTIONS, FAKE NEWS, & SOCIALISM

*Fake News is defined by the Oxford English Dictionary as "originally U.S. news that conveys or incorporates false, fabricated, or deliberately misleading information, or that is characterized as or accused of doing so."*

*The event referred to as Waco was a 51-day law enforcement siege on a compound belonging to the religious group known as the Branch Davidians. The Bureau of Alcohol, Tobacco, and Firearms (ATF) suspecting the group of stockpiling weapons obtained a search warrant for the compound and arrest warrants for the group's leader David Koresh and several other members. On February 28, 1993, when ATF attempted to serve the warrants a gunfight erupted, which resulted in the deaths of four government agents and six Branch Davidians. The FBI initiated the siege after ATFs entry on the property and failure to execute the search warrant. The siege lasted 51 days and ended on April 19, 1993, when the FBI launched an assault and initiated a tear gas attack in an attempt to force the Branch Davidians out of the ranch. During the assault, the compound became engulfed in flames. The fire resulted in the deaths of 76 Branch Davidians, including Koresh.*

*The event referred to as Ruby Ridge was an 11-day siege in 1992 that began on August 21 when U.S. Marshals attempted to apprehend and arrest Randy Weaver under a bench warrant for failing to appear on firearms charges. Weaver refused to surrender. Members of Weaver's immediate family and family friend, Kevin Harris, resisted law enforcement as well. The Hostage Rescue Team (HRT) and the FBI became involved as the siege developed. A shootout in the woods near the Weaver family's cabin involving six U.S. Marshals, Harris and Weaver's 14-year-old son resulted in the death of a U.S. Marshal and Weaver's son. Weaver's wife was killed by sniper fire during an attempted siege on the cabin. The incident was ultimately resolved by civilian negotiators. Harris surrendered and was arrested on August 30. Weaver and his three daughters surrendered the following day. The brutality of this incident was underscored by the needless shooting of the family dog.*

*The Montana Freemen was a militant "Christian Patriot" group based outside of the town of Jordan, Montana, United States. The members of the group referred to their land as "Justus Township" and had declared themselves no longer under the authority of any outside government. In 1996, the group was involved in a prolonged armed standoff with the FBI.*

---

Beauty is in the eye of the beholder. The same could be said for bias: and much has already been said, especially about the press. From this biased eye, the press struggles to put lipstick on *yellow dog democrats* posing as progressives.

The Clinton administration is best remembered for renting the Lincoln Bedroom, Monica Lewinsky, impeachment, and taking the White House china before exiting. Violent suppression of the Waco Branch Davidians, Ruby Ridge, and the Montana Freemen have largely been forgotten in classic confrontations of individual versus institution and one of the darkest chapters in our history. Using the FBI to exercise lethal force was unprecedented and avoidable.

# RUBY RIDGE INVESTIGATION

Senator Dodd recently said that the government was wasting its time "investigating Ruby Ridge and Waco Texas." Based upon what the press has offered about the standoff in Montana, the Justice Department may add the "Montana Massacre" to that list shortly.

Although the press relies heavily upon information provided by "the prosecutors," in the Montana standoff, charges against these people range from failing to display license tags to bullying the local justice of the peace. What we do know about Montana, Wyoming, and Nevada is that considerable friction exists between local ranchers and federal Fish and Wildlife agents created by enforcement of the Endangered Species and Land Management Acts. According to the National Corporation for Public Broadcasting, Fish and Wildlife agents have requested to be armed. Not unlike the Boston Tea Party or the sit-ins of the 1960s, these people's greatest crimes are their political beliefs. They are confronting a federal government that they believe is in clear violation of the first thirteen amendments.

Their lives hang in the balance.

How would this country view these acts if they were perpetrated in Beijing? Will we all "hang separately"? Senator Dodd, are we safe as long as these people are the only ones in bondage? How much longer can the Justice Department's penchant for ambivalence and brutality be ignored by the national press? Is it unreasonable to expect a Justice Department that can tolerate federal laws broken by Farrakhan in his fundraising trip to supporters of terrorism around the world, to redress grievances of families in Montana without violence?

March 28, 1996

# DUE PROCESS

*Potter Stewart was an American lawyer and judge who served as an Associate Justice on the United States Supreme Court from 1958 to 1981. Kevin Clinesmith was the FBI agent that falsified emails as justification to continue investigating "Russian Collusion." Based upon the Watergate investigation, some accountability from the DNC, Hillary Clinton, and Barack Obama would seem essential in closing this dark chapter in FBI history. Efforts by the Durham Investigation were thwarted by a D.C. jury composed of Hillary Clinton donors whose objectivity was questionable.*

---

WHEN JUSTICE STEWART WAS ASKED WHAT CONSTITUTED OBSCENITY, he gave his famous shorthand description: "I know it when I see it." Had Justice Potter been asked about FBI bias, his shorthand description would have been the same; "I know it when I see it." Swallowing camels and straining gnats, Horowitz put lipstick on "bias" and "spying" that even a pig would recognize breathing life into "What is, is" and a black eye to due process.

The Clintons spun their way out of Waco and the Davidians, Ruby Ridge, and the Montana Freemen in perhaps the bloodiest chapters of FBI history. Changing the rules for a bureaucracy with absolute power only creates loopholes that Michael Avenatti could exploit. Incarcerating those responsible for using Carter Page's life as an "insurance policy" is a better solution. Flipping Clinesmith to ultimately discover what Barack and Hillary knew and when would be a good beginning to end FBI abuses.

Unfortunately, hating Donald Trump has spawned a tyranny that suspends the rule of law. In this light, if Carter Page is in danger, we are all in danger. Without due process and the rule of law, government of the people and for the people remains in jeopardy.

December 12, 2019

# SILENCING THE VOICES OF DISSENT

*The United States started to withdraw its military forces from Afghanistan during spring 2021, intending to have all of its military forces withdrawn by September 11, 2021. There were a number of attacks by Taliban forces on evacuating U.S. troops and allied units during the following months. The last U.S. military planes left Afghanistan on August 31, 2021. The images of desperate refugees clinging to landing gears still begs the question: did it have to end like this?*

---

RECENT EVENTS IN AFGHANISTAN AND THE SOUTHERN BORDER HAVE obfuscated grievous civil rights violations in our own Capitol. Based upon news sources verified by SCOPES, this is what we know about the January 6 Trump supporters protesting election results:

Over 500 subpoenas in 40 states have been issued by the DOJ and served by the FBI as of August 26 in an ongoing nationwide dragnet relying on political informants.

Most of the charges are for: *Knowingly entering a restricted building; demonstrating in a Capitol building; disorderly conduct.*

Most of those charged are less than 30 years old and range from veterans and law enforcement officers to soccer moms and students.

It is not clear how many protestors are being held at the D.C. prison or how many are being denied habeas corpus.

On July 29th, four Republican congressmen were not allowed to visit jailed protestors.

Five people died in the protest. Three were protestors who died of natural causes in the aftermath. One protestor was shot dead by Capitol police. A Capitol police officer died in the aftermath from heart failure.

The event has been described by CNN and various WOKE media as an "Insurrection" and the participants as "conspirators."

According to U.S. News & World Report, at least one Confederate flag was seen, and the protestors had plastic handcuffs.

The event has been described by CNN and various WOKE media as an "Insurrection" and the participants as "conspirators."

According to U.S. News & World Report, at least one Confederate flag was seen, and the protestors had plastic handcuffs.

According to Mark Twain, "The difference in the right word and the almost right word is the difference in lightning and lightning bug." Controlling the rhetoric is essential to controlling the narrative: choosing *conspirator* instead of *protestor* and *insurrection* rather than *protest* justify suspension of civil rights for Trump haters. Regardless of rhetoric, citizens from 40 different states being held in the D.C. prison without due process are political prisoners. Our outrage should exceed our fear of the FBI and DOJ for in the final analysis, "If we don't all hang together, we shall surely hang separately."

August 31, 2021

# CLINTON ECONOMIC
# RECOVERY PLAN

*Breaking the back of inflation, ending the cold war, and 4.5% GDP growth ushered in a generation of prosperity and twelve years of a Republican White House. Distorting the Reagan legacy would be the first order of business for the Clintons. The cornerstone to the Reagan legacy was reduction of marginal tax rates from 78% to 28%. Tax revenues exploded, but so did spending in a Democrat Congress, by using continuing resolutions to fund special interests. Remarkably, changing the names would make these editorials relevant to the present political climate.*

---

"I PLEDGE ALLEGIANCE TO THE CLINTON ECONOMIC RECOVERY PLAN and to the prosperity and sacrifice for which it stands. We renounce Ronald Reagan, the Federal Reserve, and anybody making $50,000 a year, except lawyers and 6 o'clock evening news creators, as unpatriotic materialistic pigs."

**Professor**: Okay, class, who can tell me how Mr. Clinton will lead us out of this economic malaise?"

**Student**: "It's simple. First, you close down all the defense industries where scientists are conducting sophisticated electronic research and development projects. Second, you put price and wage controls on the entire medical industry and stop its growth dead in its track. Then you teach those doctors, scientists, and chemists who have been thrown out of work how to lay brick and mix mortar for roads and bridges."

**Professor**: "Won't this be expensive?"

**Student**: "You bet. But we will ask the people to invest in more expensive education."

**Professor**: "What about people who have to pay for real educations?"

**Student**: "Easy. Think of it as 'Reverse Investment.' When they invest in the Clinton Plan, the Educational Tuition Agency will lend them their money back."

**Professor**: "What will all of this accomplish?"

**Student**: "3% growth in Gross National Product. Tops!"

**Professor**: "What would happen if we could achieve 4.5% growth in GNP?"

February 26, 1993

# BASHING CHINA, PART 1

*In 2012, National Public Radio (NPR) published articles about activists protesting the butchering of dogs and China's labor practices. One article published on February 6, 2012, "Chinese Labor Practices Sour Apple Consumers," described Apple workers' low wages. Another article published on March 29, 2012, "Headed For The Butcher, Chinese Dogs Are Rescued," discussed changing mindsets in China related to dogs.*

---

RECENTLY, NATIONAL PUBLIC RADIO (NPR) REPORTED THAT CHINESE cuisine still included man's best friend followed by a report on Apple's wages in China, which are less than $500 per month in some cases.

In America we don't eat abandoned dogs, we euthanize them and in poorer counties throw their carcasses on garbage dumps to be devoured by scavengers. Thirty-five years ago the *Cultural Revolution* enforced by the *Red Guard* allocated all land, labor, and capital resources. There were no wages paid in China. Everyone worked for the state, and people starved. *One percent* of those were sent to factories to work until they died.

The Chinese people know much more about us than we know about them, because China TV is more objective than NPR. When scripture was being transcribed, the Chinese developed writing and domesticated seeds. Today, they admire Americans for their generosity. They have adopted our language, our music, and gratefully, our debt. Recently, ChinaOil surpassed *Exxon®* as the largest oil company in the world. They have pulled the plug on solar and wind energy subsidies in favor of nuclear energy. They have gone from bicycles to automobiles in a generation. Within the decade, China will have a larger Gross Domestic Product than the United States.

It's not clear why NPR reinforces Chinese stereotypes. Perhaps it's because Chinese artisans have depicted the Statue of Liberty in the likeness of Barack Obama holding Chairman Mao's *Redbook* in place of the Bible. Regardless, it makes vilifying the Chinese good politics.

April 9, 2012

# BASHING CHINA, PART 2

*The conflict between China and Tibet can be boiled down to the debate of whether or not the territories within the People's Republic of China claimed as Tibet should or could separate themselves from China and become a sovereign state. The cultural differences are distinct and dramatic and involve language as well as religion. The Tibetans see themselves as occupied by the Chinese. The frequent self-immolations by Buddhist monks underscore these differences. Chen Guangcheng is the blind legal dissident who sought refuge in the American Embassy in Beijing immigrating to the U.S. in 2012.*

*Author's Note: I was in Tibet when an immolation occurred. Our group was hurriedly shuttled away from the area. My visit to China predated the presidency of Xi Jinping. The people have not changed but the leadership has changed dramatically.*

―――――

BY THE TIME THIS IS PRINTED, HOPEFULLY THE WELL-ORCHESTRATED Blind Chinese Dissident Event (BCDE) will have only become another colossal embarrassment to the national media and state department.

Following the collapse of the Cultural Revolution and the Red Guard Reign of Terror in 1984, Chinese leaders were faced with a population explosion with millions on the brink of starvation. The one-child policy was a desperate measure spawned to accommodate desperate circumstances. (Think of the Great Depression on steroids!) It is not Chinese law. As Party policy, violators will lose Party favor and public sector jobs, much like party patronage in this country, except that it is less pervasive. Chinese law forbids forced abortion much like U.S. law forbids forced sterilization. The policy does not apply to farm families.

Chinese policy makers have taken a country on the verge of starvation and turned it into a poster child for free market allocation of resources. They have not only raised living standards dramatically but also produced enough surplus to keep Americans in a lifestyle that we can no longer afford. If the rest of the world could make the same progress the Chinese have made in human rights since the *Red Guard Reign of Terror*, Middle East atrocities would become history.

Tibetans will testify that China is unwelcome in their country. Adopting a policy of common decency toward China might lend our concern for Tibetans a more sincere quality. Who do our policy makers think Americans are by pointing out the splinter in China's eye when we have a log in our own? Except for Europe's plunge into World War I, America's exhibition of incompetence, hubris, and ignorance in the *BCDE* is unprecedented.

May 3, 2012

# OBAMAGANDA

*In 2009, General Motors filed for Chapter 11 bankruptcy, which permits the reorganization of a business under the bankruptcy laws of the United States. They received $33 billion in debtor-in-possession financing to remain in operation until all major assets were sold and the corporation was liquidated.*

---

WHO SAYS GOVERNMENT CAN'T CREATE JOBS?! GOVERNMENT MOTORS (formerly General Motors) is hiring 4,000 laid-off workers and it only cost taxpayers $46,000,000,000. Since $23,000,000,000 has already been repaid, add a little interest, and that's hardly $6,000,000 per job. Just in the nick of time too, the U.S. Postal Service lost $2.2 billion in the first quarter of 2011 and is on course to reach its borrowing limit of $15 billion by yearend. How can the post office lose so much money when nobody uses it anymore? According to the U.S. Postal Service, *billions are needed to provide healthcare benefits for future retirees!!!!* No wonder *Joe Sixpack* can't afford decent healthcare!

You think this is insanity?! Postal revenues have been in a steady decline for twenty years! If these resources were allocated by the marketplace, *UPS* and *FedEx* would be delivering the mail with health benefits and a profit!!!

You think *this* is scary?! Postal revenues account for less than 0.01% of GDP. Healthcare accounts for 16% of GDP. If it costs the government $6,000,000 to *SAVE* one job and $15 billion to maintain a business nobody uses, what will the cost of an office visit be in ten years under Obamacare?

Oh well, maybe it'll be different this time!

May 11, 2011

# QUANTIFYING GOOD HEALTH

*Patient Protection and Affordable Care Act, also known as the Affordable Care Act (ACA) or Obamacare is a federal statute signed into law by former President Barack Obama in 2010.*

———

IF WE AGREE THAT PATIENTS CANNOT AFFORD THE HEALTHCARE SYSTEM we have today, instituting universal healthcare would hardly seem to resolve the problem. Masking the cost of healthcare with government reimbursement results in the perception that health-care is *free*. If the rules of supply and demand have not been repealed, demands upon the system would overwhelm it.

In addition to paying people when they are sick, paying people when they are well should be part of any comprehensive solution. No one is naïve enough to believe that people will start exercising and stop their daily intake of fried potatoes and ice cream. Nonetheless, quantifying the worth of good health would go a long way toward reassessing the value of good health.

Such a system already exists. *High-deductible* health insurance policies coupled with *Health Savings Accounts* should be part of any comprehensive solution to healthcare delivery. *High-deductible* healthcare insurance requires the patient to pay all medical bills up to $3,500 annually. By using *high-deductible* health insurance policies, premiums are lowered and with the savings from premium costs, *Health Savings Accounts* can be funded to reduce high-deductibility exposure. Using tax credits for individuals or businesses would cover the balance. The Health Savings Account *quantifies the value of good health* each time someone weighs a decision to deplete their passbook savings to use the healthcare system.

This solution does not work well for the chronically sick. For healthy younger people, *Health Savings Accounts* will not only *quantify the value of good health* but also pay for the chronically sick and provide a retirement supplement for a bankrupt social security program.

December 4, 2007

# HOW MUCH DOES THE FREE LUNCH COST?

*Patient Protection and Affordable Care Act, also known as the Affordable Care Act (ACA) or Obamacare is a federal statute signed into law by former President Barack Obama in 2010. As Nancy Pelosi famously said of the 2,000 page law, "Nobody really knows what's in there."*

———————

ENTITLEMENTS ARE A CRUEL HOAX PROMOTED BY SINISTER POLITICIANS who have made a mockery of the notion that government should be "for the people." Somebody must pay for the "free lunch."

Insurance premiums are based upon age and deductibles: the higher the deductible, the lower the premium by actuarial statistics. In other words, raising the deductible to equal the cost of the policy would reduce the cost of the policy dramatically. For example, a $7,000 policy with a $1,000 deductible converted to a $7,000 deductible would cost about $2,000. In short, choosing to pay the doctor rather than the insurance company results in substantial insurance savings.

Choosing to pay neither the doctor nor the insurance company requires a healthy lifestyle. Diabetes, lung cancer, and heart disease can be prevented with changes in lifestyle. Such changes would reduce the demand for healthcare and subsequently the cost of healthcare.

No one should be exposed to the financial burden inherent with genetic predispositions or catastrophic health events. Removing the federal government from the administration of healthcare and insurance companies from the billing of healthcare should more than pay unanticipated costs arising from converting insurance premiums to deductibles.

Masked in compassion for the uninsured, Obamacare is the cruelest hoax of all. For professional politicians depending upon the stupidity of the American public, Obamacare will become the sweetest political payoff since Medicaid and a regulators' dream come true.

March 28, 2017

# "HOODOO ECONOMICS"
## CLINTONOMICS

*Voodoo or Hoodoo Economics is defined by Lexico.com as "an economic policy perceived as being unrealistic and ill-advised, in particular a policy of maintaining or increasing levels of public spending while reducing taxation." The unflattering term was popularized by a critical press to describe "supply side" economic policy during the Reagan and Bush administrations. Simply put, tax revenues would increase by lowering tax rates. Supply side economics is credited with the generational prosperity legacy of the Reagan administration.*

*"Clintonomics" refers to the economic policies put in place by former President Bill Clinton during his two terms. More socialistic in nature, these policies appealed to the central planners and a more socialistic approach to resource allocation.*

———

FOR EVERYBODY WHO BELIEVES THAT GOVERNOR CLINTON CAN CREATE jobs, there's some good news and some bad news.

"Give me the good news first."

If your job is in the defense industry, there is no good news. If your job is in the drug and healthcare industry, Governor Clinton doesn't like the profitability of this segment of our economy, and he has promised to cripple the industry with price controls as soon as possible. (The Japanese are ecstatic!)

"So what do we get? Garth Brooks on every stereo and a *penthouse* in every mailbox?"

While Governor Clinton's a little fuzzy on what he deems essential to our future economy, Senator Gore's disdain for all industry as ecological disasters is a matter of public record. Perhaps the good news is that government can create jobs. Based upon the latest statistics, it costs Uncle Sam $35,000 to create a $20,000 job.

"I'm no H&R Block, but this sounds more like 'Voodoo' economics." It's called "industrial engineering," and the concept is based upon a mentality of "If you build it they will come." "Has this worked anywhere?"

Not for long. It's been tried in a rubble of bankrupt countries, Mexico, Russia, Ethiopia, Latin America, Cuba, East Germany, North Korea, among others. "Just what we need, 'Hoodoo Economics' to replace 'Voodoo Economics.'"

October 20, 1992

# CHAPTER IV

## TARHEEL ENVY, AFRO-CENTRICITY, & STATE SUPPORTED ENTERPRISES (SSES)

# OBAMAJOBS

*Bobby Ray "Bob" Etheridge is an American politician who was the U.S. representative for North Carolina's 2nd congressional district from 1997 to 2011. He previously served as a county commissioner, state representative and state superintendent of public instruction. A member of the Democratic Party, in 2012 he was an unsuccessful candidate for the Democratic nomination for Governor of North Carolina.*

*Beverly Eaves Perdue is an American businesswoman, politician, and member of the Democratic Party who served as the 73rd Governor of North Carolina from 2009 to 2013.*

*The first female governor of North Carolina, Perdue started her political career in the 1980s, serving in the North Carolina House of Representatives. After serving five terms in the North Carolina Senate, she was elected as the 32nd Lieutenant Governor of North Carolina.*

*On January 26, 2012, facing sinking approval ratings, Perdue announced that she would not seek reelection in the 2012 gubernatorial election. She left office in January 2013 under allegations of questionable policies and a Blue tidal wave ushering in the first Republican general assembly since Reconstruction.* The New York Times *characterized this historical event as the "Decline of North Carolina." In July of 2022, CNBC recognized North Carolina as* **the best state to do business.**

---

THE DAILY MANTRA *"GOVERNMENT IS CREATING JOBS"* IS BROADCAST with mind-numbing regularity as unemployment in North Carolina soars to historical levels. Even the Honorable Bobby Etheridge and Bev Perdue, the *Queens of Concrete*, are busy *creating jobs* by building roads and bridges to nowhere and giving business tax rebates to hire people for jobs that don't exist. With marching orders to keep pushing *"change you can believe in,"* how long will real job holders be able to pay for *Obamajobs* especially at these prices?!

Circa 2010

# MADISON AVENUE TAR HEELS

*Beverly Eaves Purdue is an American businesswoman, politician, and member of the Democratic Party who served as the 73rd Governor of North Carolina from 2009 to 2013.*

*On June 12, 2011, Purdue vetoed the state's $19.5 billion budget proposal, which includes big cuts to health, public safety and education, including early learning. The fiscal responsibility of the General Assembly is often credited for paving the way to make North Carolina the #1 state to do business, according to CNBC.*

---

WHY IS IT WHEN THE DEMOCRATIC NATIONAL COMMITTEE PORTRAYS North Carolinians, we sound like a cross between Goober and Barney, unable to speak a complete sentence without using *ain't!* Ironically, the latest Madison Avenue pornographic propaganda is directed at the General Assembly for failing to maintain the staggering cost of higher education, even though the cost of higher education in this state has risen faster than a barrel of West Texas Crude in the past ten years.

In an economic environment that has brought hardship to everyone in the private sector, the private sector can no longer afford *dedicated public administrators* making six-figure salaries, benefits, and pensions. Any educator who can spell *Greece* should understand why. Nonetheless, in the firm belief that bad policy makes good politics, Governor Perdue has dragged her corruption-tainted office to a new ethical low. Governor Perdue does not wish to save education: she wishes to save *educators.*

As Minnesota, Indiana, New Jersey, Wisconsin, Texas, and California try to reduce a bloated public sector dependent upon an overregulated, overtaxed private sector, the Governor is hanging desperately to the hope *you can fool 51% of the people some of the time* with enough TV advertising.

And what are the chances of success for the Democrat Club? About the same as Herbert Hoover's!!!!

June 20, 2011

# THE COUNCIL OF DECEIT:
# THINKING BIG

*In 2011, North Carolina Governor Beverly Perdue issued the Report of the Governor's Scientific Advisory Panel on Offshore Energy, including a section on wind power and the environmental impact on North Carolina.*

---

HAVE YOU HEARD THE GOOD NEWS? THE GOVERNOR AND THE Council of State are thinking big again!!! Windmills are coming to North Carolina and bringing:

- 400 new jobs.
- $1,000,000 per year to the landowners.
- Enough electricity to supply 55,000 homes.

This could be the best idea since the Southport International Seaport.

So what's not to like?

Plenty! Besides the adverse environmental impact to waterfowl as well as sound and visual pollution to pristine coastal land-scapes, wind power costs about three times as much as power generated from natural gas. The average increase in utility bills alone could amount to $500 a year. Multiply that times 55,000 and that's about $70,000/job.

Wait a minute? Isn't this just another tax in disguise?

Bingo, dumb taxpayer! Besides the lottery, gasoline tax, personal income tax, corporate tax, sales tax, you can add the *windmill tax*!!! And we're still $1.5 billion short.

Affectionately known as the *Queen of Concrete*, our governor can now add her new moniker: *Queen of Deceit*.

February 3, 2011

# BIG-TIME ACADEMICS

*In 2011, officials at the University of North Carolina raised tuition and fees by 40%. Students paid 40% more in 2011 than they paid in 2008. From 2001 to 2011, tuition increased 150%.*

---

THE PRICE OF BIG TIME ACADEMICS IS GOING UP—ABOUT 40% AT THE flagship. (That's the one in Chapel Hill, not the one where they played basketball for President Obama recently.) In round numbers that's about $2, 400 per student, and the flagship doesn't even make a profit, which should please the politically correct academic zombies of *Occupy Wall Street/Chapel Hill/Wilmington*.

On the other hand, Duke Power needs a 17% rate hike to cover escalating fuel costs, because the politically correct Obama administration will not permit infrastructure necessary to reduce escalating fuel costs or the 20,000 jobs it would create. The rate increase will cost the consumer about $100 per year, and that includes a little profit.

What's wrong with this picture?

How come Duke Power can get along on a 17% increase and Joe Six-Pack on unemployment benefits while *UNC Big Time Academicians* glibly raise tuition 40%? Why does it cost so much more to turn out kids who are brain dead upon graduation? Not too long ago you could get a good *dedicated public servant* for less than $100,000 per year.

The University has come a long way since C.D. Spangler was the president—about $6,000 per semester. Scorners seem justified when they sneered at the image of the *oldest state-supported university*. UNC is not the oldest state supported university, it's just the latest university supported by the Student Loan Administration in Washington.

November 14, 2011

# DEBUNKING EHRMAN

*Bart Denton Ehrman is an American New Testament scholar who focuses on textual criticism of the New Testament, the historical Jesus, and the origins and development of early Christianity. The author and editor of 30 books, including three college textbooks, he has also authored six* New York Times *bestsellers. He is the James A. Gray Distinguished Professor of Religious Studies at the University of North Carolina at Chapel Hill. Convinced "what ye seek in the Bible, ye shall find," critics have accused Ehrman of taking poetic license with scripture much like Chernow and history. Both have been enormously successful in this approach to their fields.*

*Dr. Boyd was a professor of Religious Studies during the 1960s at the University of North Carolina, emphasizing Old Testament and New Testament study. His lectures were intriguing and delivered with a riveting flare. His lecture hall held 300 and was always full.*

---

In the movie *Oh God* (circa 1985), God is asked by a TV evangelist about his role in revealing *the true word of God*. God, played by George Burns, replies: *"If you want to get rich, sell Earth Shoes."* Today that would translate to Crocs instead of Earth Shoes, but is still good advice for Bart Ehrman, bestselling author and latest religious shock jock at UNC-Chapel Hill.

Ehrman's shameless exploitation of Sunday school theology is symptomatic of an academic system that holds those professors in high esteem who garner lucrative grants or write something that gets published. This system perpetuates an academic status quo by leaving students with huge government loans and very limited problem-solving skills.

Before Ehrman was born, Dr. Boyd taught bible studies at UNC-Chapel Hill. His popularity was legendary and his classes were only available to upper-classmen and when guests attended on Saturdays, there was standing room only. From Dr. Boyd we learned that Jonah was swallowed by a whale. Perhaps the story was an allegory. Many theologians believed that the story of Jonah was the unerring word of God; others believed that the story was divinely inspired. Perhaps the story was one man's attempt to escape the deity. He never told us what he thought.

Dr. Boyd probably never garnered lucrative grants for the university. I would wager that he never got rich by teaching Bible at UNC. We didn't know it at the time but Dr. Boyd was on a far more important mission—he was teaching us *how to think* rather than *what to think*.

March 29, 2009

# AFRO-CENTRICITY

*In 2019, at a number of campuses, including the University of North Carolina at Chapel Hill, the University of Wisconsin at Madison, Roger Q. Mills Elementary in Dallas, the University of Minnesota, and Bowling Green State University in Ohio, buildings and schools named after people with ties to the Ku Klux Klan were renamed. Many were renamed as a result of protests. The Ku Klux Klan, commonly shortened to the KKK or the Klan, is an American group. Critical thinkers question the validity of these accusations noting the purpose of the early Ku Klux Klan and its evolution into something quite different and site Governor Aycock as an example.*

---

IN A 1993 TIME MAGAZINE ARTICLE, DR. MARY LEFKOWITZ, professor of humanities at Wellesley College, believed that Afro-Centric history "substitutes pseudo history for the real thing." Nonetheless, Afro-Centric history is noticeably fashionable at UNC and Duke, among other politically correct institutions. Such teaching has fostered the idea that North Carolina is not the only state in the South that is dealing with the legacy of racism.

The Republican Party of Lincoln was deeply divided between reconciliation and revenge. The goodwill established at Appomattox died with Lincoln's assassination and the impeachment of Vice President Johnson. Civil rights were the first casualty of occupation. Retribution and lawlessness followed, as victors divided the carcass of the vanquished. Ironically, the KKK was born to restore civil rights egregiously taken as spoils of war reminiscent of the Black Panther Movement almost a hundred years later.

Renaming buildings because their namesakes were members of the KKK amounts to a twenty-first century book burning. For 'isms,' Communism, Nazism, Environmentalism, to flourish, history must be rewritten to accommodate tyrannical agendas. The South does not suffer from a legacy of racism any more than New York or California. The South suffers from a legacy of occupation.

October 20, 2019

# DOOK'S ROOTS

*The rates of tuition at American colleges and universities have been rising yearly. Duke University is a private research university in Durham, North Carolina. In 1980, a year's tuition at Duke cost $4,230. In 1990, the cost went up to $12,800. By 1999, the year this editorial was written, a year at Duke cost $22,420 (not including room and board). As of the publication of this book in 2022, a year's tuition at Duke will cost students $60,435. (My apology to my beautiful daughter-in-law, Carol, who has learned to tolerate her UNC surroundings.)*

---

NORTH CAROLINIANS SHOULD BE PROUD OF DUKE UNIVERSITY. Tuition now exceeds $31,000 per year just like the Ivy Leagues. SAT entrance requirements have been raised to 1,600 plus or minus $31,000. Parents from New Jersey who think that their children are attending Stanford should not only be proud of *Duke's* meteoric rise in the tuition race, they should also be rich.

Uncle Kirk went to Duke before J.B. Duke bequeathed his tar and nicotine fortune. Back then it was called *Trinity College,* and

Uncle Kirk played trombone at the Sigma Chi House to pay tuition *and* living expenses. I can still hear Uncle Kirk leading the *T.C. Victory Cheer* prior to every Duke football game!

*Ah-dee, ah-dee, ah-dee Y! T-R-I-N-I-T-Y.*
*Trinity, Trinity, that's our cry. Go-o-o Trinity!*

March 15, 1999

# SUBSIDIZING INCOMES OF DEDICATED PUBLIC SERVANTS

*James "J.C." Moeser, was the former Chancellor Emeritus from 2000 to 2008 and served as Interim Director of the Institute for Arts and Humanities at the University of North Carolina at Chapel Hill (UNC-CH) from 2016 to 2017.*

*In 2022, during a live-streamed panel that was hosted by the Coalition for Carolina, Moeser, along with several other former figureheads at UNC-CH, expressed concern about partisan politics negatively impacting UNC-CH's Board of Trustees—and therefore, impacting the policies at UNC-CH itself.*

*The skyrocketing costs of tuition and jaw dropping administrative costs have not gone unnoticed by citizens with family incomes of $40 thousand a year who can no longer afford to send their children to UNC-CH. They argue the University has lost its mission as the Oldest State-Supported University.*

―――――

## DEDICATED PUBLIC SERVANTS

UNC-CH IS IN A LOT OF TROUBLE ACCORDING TO J.C. MOESER, former UNC-CH chancellor, and Board of Trustees' chairman. Even though applications are up, state funding is up, alumni giving is up; professorial salaries and chancellor's incomes are up but not enough. Faculty and administrative salaries rose only 15% during the pandemic and N.C. taxpayers need to subsidize a life-style comparable to Duke and other prestigious universities. According to Moeser, if the present NC-Chapel Hill Board of Trustees chairman David Boliek would acknowledge the critical roll teachers, staff, and administrators play and let them run the university, teachers, staff, and administrative salaries could go up by 30%. Boliek needs to trust "faculty, staff, & administrators to run the university."

Moeser is a modern day "dedicated public servant". Armed with a degree in music and a major in organ playing, Moeser hit the Chancellor jackpot when he left Cornhusker University for Blue Heaven Political Correctness where he surrounded himself by Trumphaters, the rich, and the famous, subsisting on a salary exceeding $500K. It was his mission to provide *moral and ethical leadership* that would change North Carolina and indeed the South.

Moral and ethical leadership notwithstanding, the University is a multi-billion dollar conglomerate. Trusting the fiscal wellbeing of the university to faculty that could not run a lemonade stand would be fiscal suicide. Moral and ethical leadership would be better served by recognizing the disparity between *dedicated public servant* income and the tribute N.C. citizens are expected to pay for that disparity.

Self-adulation for allowing mob rule to remove Silent Sam from campus did not change North Carolina, much less the South. The names of those who truly changed North Carolina have been removed from campus.

*"We must educate not only ourselves but see to it that the negro has an opportunity for education. As a white man I am afraid of but one thing for my race and that is that we shall become afraid to give the negro a fair chance. The first duty of every man is to develop himself to the uttermost and the only limitation upon his duty is that he shall take pains to see that in his own development he does no injustice to those beneath him. This is true of races as well as of individuals. Considered properly it is not a limitation but a condition of development. The white man in the South can never attain to his fullest growth until he does absolute justice to the negro race."*

—The Education Governor Charles B. Aycock, circa 1903

March 4, 2022

# POLITICAL CORRECTNESS

*The Endangered Species Act of 1973 (ESA or "The Act"; 16 U.S.C. §
1531 et seq.) is the primary law in the United States for protecting
imperiled species. Designed to protect critically imperiled species from
extinction as a "consequence of economic growth and development
untempered by adequate concern and conservation", the ESA was signed
into law by President Richard Nixon on December 28, 1973. Ironically,
critics argue the laws designed to protect endangered species have caused
the destruction of endangered as well as indigenous species.*

HAVE YOU EVER WONDERED WHY FOREST FIRES CANNOT BE PREVENTED
in California? Federal forests must adhere to the Endangered
Species Act. How many species, endangered or otherwise, must
be sacrificed at the altar of political correctness?

---

HAVE YOU EVER WONDERED WHY CALIFORNIANS WOULD RATHER
watch a forest go up in smoke than allow loggers to remove one

plank for the homeless? Probably, the same twisted logic that would watch maritime forests fall into the ocean and turtle sanctuaries destroyed because of careless sand management.

The issue of managing our natural resources responsibly is in direct conflict with the notion that taking property from the private sector and turning it into a national forest will somehow benefit us all. With proper harvests, enough wood could be saved from the ravages of forest fires to fill the needs of Habitat for Humanity forever. With proper sand management, North Carolina beaches would become turtle sanctuaries once again and 1,000-year-old maritime forests would be saved as pristine sand beaches accreted seaward.

The issue is not the cost of environmental stewardship. The issue is as old as the Constitution and the peculiar notion "all men are created with…certain inalienable rights…among these…are life, liberty, and property."

January 22, 2001

# UNELECTED &
# UNACCOUNTABLE

*The National Collegiate Athletic Association (NCAA) is an organization that focuses on regulating issues surrounding college athletes.*

*Given the amount of influence the NCAA holds over student athletes, and the large amount of revenue that athletic programs bring to universities and the NCAA (and therefore to the states in which the universities reside), there has been increasing levels of concern from both sides of the aisle about the NCAA's potential political impact. The success of public university athletic programs is essential to the ability to offer scholarships under Title IX. Public universities cannot compete with the endowments of private institutions who disdain "Big Time" athletic programs while they enjoy exemption from Title IX. In short, the athletic field levels the endowment field.*

*In recent years, the NCAA was also involved in investigations at the University of North Carolina (UNC) pertaining to allegations of academic dishonesty and fraud among student athletes, though the NCAA did not find evidence of wrongdoing. However, given that the NCAA is not responsible for making academic standards for university, some speculated that the NCAA did not have a reason to investigate this issue since the allegations had already been investigated and addressed by UNC.*

---

THE EPIDEMIC OF OPIOID ADDICTION IN MARYLAND WAS UNDERSCORED by the remarks of the President of that University. The NCAA's political interference into North Carolina's legislative process is unprecedented and raises serious questions about the prolonged investigation of UNC athletics.

Composed of academic wonks drawing absurd incomes at taxpayer and ticket-holder expense, the NCAA board of governors has now embraced political correctness for the core value of respect for institutional autonomy and philosophical differences. The opaque orthodoxy embraced by political correctness does not tolerate political or philosophical dissent and raises serious questions about the NCAA's political agenda and how they will allocate future revenues. How does the Board feel about the name Washington & Lee? If the University of Maryland wanted to teach a history course in Southern Reconstruction, would this trigger an NCAA boycott?

Enriched by television revenues generated by championship basketball, the NCAA has become a cesspool of philosophical intolerance boasting 500 employees that assure safe, healthy, and discrimination-free atmosphere. Holding the University that fostered Dean Smith hostage is the height of hypocrisy and a frightful example of more power than good women should want or bad men should have.

April 13, 2017

# TO SEEM RATHER THAN TO BE

*In 2010, there was an investigation into the UNC football program, involving improper player contacts with professional sports agents and other outsiders and also possible academic misconduct. In 2011, Butch Davis, who had survived the most dangerous days of the NCAA investigation, was fired from his position. The announcement was made by UNC Chancellor Holden Thorp.*

*The N.C. state motto is: To Be Rather Than to Seem.*

THIRTEEN MONTHS AGO, THE NCAA ALERTED UNC OF NINE MAJOR rule infractions involving the UNC football program. At that time, Chancellor Thorp and Athletic Director Baddour wisely avoided a kneejerk rush to judgment of Coach Davis and launched an extensive investigation of their own that uncovered an academic impropriety that they reported to the NCAA. Last week, after thirteen months of subpoenas, exoneration of the tutor, a lawsuit, three court appearances securing privileged correspondence, Honor

Court, and NCAA investigation, Butch Davis was fired after *no evidence was found to directly link him to the NCAA violations.*

We know very little about Holden except that he is young and that he sends sophomoric emails from time to time. We know less about the *dedicated public servants du jour* serving as *UNC Board Members.* Hopefully, neither was directly linked to the NCAA allegations.

We do know something about Butch. When he arrived, the UNC football program was in disarray. Since that time, Butch has fought personal battles with the tenacity of Kay Yow and Jim Valvano. The NCAA did not intimidate or deter him from his promise to bring excellence to UNC's football program. Last year's team will long be remembered for their tenacity in the face of withering adversity. What they lacked in experience and talent, they made up for in uncommon determination to prevail. The victory over Tennessee personified their tenacious character.

Coach Davis kept his promise to the University not only in terms of wins and losses but also by instilling values that his players will use long after football is over. In return, Holden Thorp and the Board have demonstrated deceit and dishonesty dangling Davis for thirteen months and then cutting the rope. It is not clear how the University's image will benefit from their pious decision to hold Coach Davis to higher standards of behavior than they require of themselves.

August 2, 2011

# BICENTENNIAL FOOTNOTE

*Frank Porter Graham was an American educator and political activist. He was elected President of the University of North Carolina at Chapel Hill in 1930, and he later became the first President of the consolidated University of North Carolina system.*

*In 1979, Joseph A. Califano, Jr., then Secretary of Health, Education and Welfare, announced administrative action against University at Chapel Hill for admission policies Mr. Califano believed were racially biased.*

*William Loeb was publisher of the* Manchester Union Leader *for many years and was known as the King Maker because New Hampshire held the first primaries. To have editorials printed, subscription to the paper was required. Mr. Loeb gave the author a subscription to fulfill this requirement. When he died, he left his publication to his employees.*

I WONDER IF DR. FRANK PORTER GRAHAM WOULD HAVE BEEN SO solicitous of the present administration in light of the previous democratic administration's effort to cut the university's history to

186 years. From the *Manchester Union Leader* addressed to William Loeb:

> "Today, Joe Califano will try to close the doors of the oldest state supported university in the country. Although poor by sister colony standards, North Carolinians were first to agree to divide their wealth to insure access to higher education for all citizens regardless of economic status. Because of their foresight, the University has continued to provide quality education and open doors of opportunity to those who could not afford private educations.
>
> "The same North Carolinians who established the university refused to ratify the Constitution because they feared a powerful central government. To be sure if public prayer threatens the principle of separation of church and state, Joe Califano is a threat to the integrity of public education and a frightening revelation of 'More power than good men should want or bad men should have.'"

March 23, 1979

# SOME THINGS ARE PRICELESS

*On July 9, 2019, the editorial board of the* New York Times *published an editorial entitled "The Decline of North Carolina."*

---

## THE GOOD OLD NORTH STATE

THE NEW YORK TIMES ARTICLE ENTITLED "THE DECLINE OF NORTH Carolina" blames the present economic chaos in Raleigh on the Party of Lincoln and Reagan, lambasting North Carolinians for diversity of political thought. Ironically the decline of this vulnerable bastion of yellow journalism is second only to the decline of the New York public school system.

Using talking points from MoveOn.org email blasts and the Dukes of Hazzard as resource material, these purveyors of propaganda have stereotyped the Almighty's anointed as gun-totin' rednecks with speech impediments. If lucky, this cesspool of narrow minded, ill-mannered damnyankees will become carpetbaggers, escape crime and pollution, and retire in North Carolina!

*Though scorners may sneer at*
*And Whittlings defame her,*
*Still my heart fills with gladness Whenever we name her...*
*Hurrah, Hurrah*
*The Good Old North State Forever*

---

## SOME THINGS ARE PRICELESS

NEW YORKERS ARE TRULY DIFFERENT FROM NORTH CAROLINIANS. IF this were not so, everyone would have drowned in the Hudson River plane crash had only New Yorkers been aboard. Common courtesy aside, there are other deep cultural differences.

They don't call it the Big Apple for nothing. They boast the largest concentration of fruitcakes on the planet.

New Yorkers are somewhat delusional. For example, they think the New York Giants play football in New York, Al Gore discovered the Internet, and Mayor Bloomberg was a Republican. More recently, New Yorkers believe Pottygate will get PayPal® to Wall Street and prodigal democrats in charge again. New Yorkers are gullible. They have forsaken the Holy Scripture in preference for thumping the *New York Times* on which they rely for talking points. They believe Forrest Gump, the Dukes of Hazzard, and Gomer Pyle are real people.

New Yorkers have a high tolerance for losers: Knicks, Mets, Jets, Giants, Yankees, Buffalo, and Syracuse. In the spirit of Bull Run, Antietam, and Cold Harbor, North Carolina has the Panthers, the Tar Heels, and Ol' Roy.

New Yorkers are big timers and big spenders. New York is expensive!!!!

North Carolina is priceless.

January 2013

# DREDGED MATERIAL
# MISMANAGEMENT PLAN

*In Carteret County, North Carolina, there is a Dredged Material Management Plan (DMMP) for the Morehead City Harbor designed to keep sand within the littoral system. Previous to this principle, the United States Corps of Engineers primary mission was to keep Beaufort Inlet navigable at artificial depths in the least cost manner possible. Maintaining Beaufort Inlet at artificial depths began to erode Bogue Banks as early as the 60s by removing sand from the littoral system starving beaches to Bogue Inlet. In Pilkey's book,* How to live with an island: A handbook to Bogue Banks, North Carolina, *he acknowledges this phenomenon. Later, as a recognized expert on beach erosion, he adopted the mantra "Retreat from the Shoreline," and blamed erosion on sea level rise, island migration, and major storm events. Thanks to the efforts of numerous organizations, today the first line of stable vegetation on Bogue Banks is 100 yards seaward since 1987.*

---

IF YOU DON'T LIVE IN CARTERET COUNTY OR OWN A MORTGAGE there, you probably don't recognize the acronym DMMP. It stands for Dredged Material Management Plan and outlines what Bogue Banks and Morehead City Harbor will look like in twenty years. If enacted, DMMP will affect every citizen in North Carolina.

Morehead City Harbor is one of numerous State Supported Enterprises (SSEs) that dot the map of North Carolina. They are the mother's milk of professional politicians who create votes in the name of "creating jobs." Contrived by people who could not run a lemonade stand, the twenty-year DMMP will cost billions of state and federal dollars and achieve little change in income. By using fifty-year depreciation schedules and revenue projections that would require the closing of Norfolk, Charleston, and Savannah seaports to achieve, the politicians who concocted this scheme will be long gone when the tax bill comes due for North Carolinians. As a taxpayer, you are the investor of last resort and the underwriters are immune from prosecution.

The most frightening part of the DMMP will require taking Beaufort Inlet at 54 feet from 45 feet. The dry beach avulsion resulting from this dredging will be immediate, permanent, and devastating—causing catastrophic environmental damage along the entire length of Bogue Banks. Sea turtle habitats, seafood estuaries, maritime forests, and a property tax base that has grown from $675,000 in 1967 to over $5 billion in 2012 will be lost.

In summary, SSEs are the most insidious tax increases that North Carolinians have to bear, taxes that stifle entrepreneurs and the imagination to start small businesses that professional politicians disdain. For the unemployed and the underemployed, SSEs are political tricks of giving false hope where none exists.

January 14, 2014

# BEING GREEN

*On March 26, 2009, the Southern Environmental Law Center shared a press release stating the Environmental Protection Agency (EPA) determined that PCS phosphate mining was creating environmental harm in Beaufort County, North Carolina.*

---

*"A government big enough to give you everything you want, is big enough to take away everything you have."*
  —Thomas Jefferson

*"Government's view of the economy could be summed up in a few short phrases: If it moves, tax it. If it keeps moving, regulate it. And if it stops moving, subsidize it."*
  —Ronald Reagan

AFTER 40 YEARS OF MINING PHOSPHATE, THE FUTURE OF BEAUFORT County's largest employer is being threatened by the Environmental Protection Agency (EPA) if PCS Phosphate can't satisfy wetland and river concerns. How do you quantify the cost of this regulation?

Look at it this way. After fifteen years, the North Carolina Council of Economic Advisors has invested over $350,000,000 in the Global TransPark. In the past fifty years, the North Carolina Ports Authority has invested similar amounts in the Morehead City Harbor Project. Assuming that the Global TransPark will be wildly successful over the next five years, the net increase in jobs in eastern North Carolina will be zero.

What are the benefits if EPA will be successful in their efforts? Wetlands about the size of a football field!

Add carbon-emission regulations and taxes on utilities and automobiles, pretty soon we will be talking about real jobs, real people, and an economy going nowhere. It's a lot easier *being green* these days but a lot more expensive.

April 17, 2009

# THE MISERY INDEX

*The Organization of the Petroleum Exporting Countries (OPEC) is an international organization comprised of over a dozen countries worldwide. Founded in 1960 in Baghdad, Iraq, its ultimate goal is helping OPEC countries, all of which exported large amounts of petroleum, establish and maintain secure local economies. During the Nixon presidency, OPEC weaponized its oil production to punish the U.S. for its Mideast policies which resulted in long lines at the pump and an inflationary spiral that lasted until the Reagan administration in 1982.*

*Nearly two years after the COVID-19 pandemic began, the Build Back Better Act was introduced as part of President Joe Biden's Build Back Better Plan. The bill, which was initially proposed to cost $3.5 trillion, focused on economic recovery as well as climate change provisions and social policies (particularly those focused on healthcare and childcare).*

*After negotiation, the bill was passed in the House of Representatives, though the cost was lowered from $3.5 trillion to $2.2 trillion.*

*Following the bill and statements from President Biden suggesting that there was a need for increased oil production, OPEC responded hesitantly, noting that major changes in supply and demand could have*

*negative consequences on OPEC countries' economies. The unintended*
*consequences of BBB and dependence on foreign oil have resulted in an*
*inflationary spiral not seen since Ronald Reagan took office 50 years ago.*

———

CONVINCING   THE   PUBLIC   THAT   STOPPING   THE   CLIMATE   FROM
changing was essential to national security, the Obama administration set about distorting the accomplishments of the Reagan
administration to justify radical Obama/Biden economic policies.
Today, the Biden/(Obama) administration policies are inflicting
global suffering.

Following the Nixon and Carter economic policies dictated by
OPEC, President Reagan inherited a 19% misery index (Unemployment + Inflation Rate) with unemployment at 7.2%. Price and
wage controls and reckless government spending served to make
the problem worse. The economy, as reflected by the Dow Jones
Industrials, had not exceeded its previous high of 1,000 in over 8
years! Fed Chairman Volcker warned Reagan the policies necessary to correct two administrations' profligate economic policies
would inflict severe political pain on Reagan and economic pain
on the entire population.

Inflation stood at 14% in April 1980. The federal funds rate
peaked at 20% a year later. The price of oil and gold plummeted:
the U.S.S.R. went bankrupt, fear of Japan's economic juggernaut
gripped the nation as China opened its economy to free markets.
Reagan lost the congress in 1982 in the wake of monetary policy
that put the economy into an induced coma. By the end of his
administration, the Dow Jones doubled, inflation dropped to 1.5%,
and unemployment hovered around 3.5% ushering in a generation of prosperity and Dow Jones exceeding 20,000.

Today, we have an 8% inflation rate and an unemployment rate
of 3.5%. The federal funds rate is negligible, and the Fed window
is wide open. Until the Fed funds rate exceeds the misery index,

the evils playing out in Ukraine will only get worse. "Being behind the curve" in monetary policy portends a grim future for the economy: $20 bread and 10% interest rates. ***Build Back Better*** would be economic Armageddon risking hyperinflation, scarcity, and ultimately economic depression rending the very fabric of our society.

March 10, 2022

# CONVERTING SILK TO A SOW'S EAR!!!

*In 2011, Governor Beverly Perdue debated whether PCS Phosphate would be able to build a sulfur-melting plant at the North Carolina state port. Fortunately, cooler heads prevailed.*

———

LET ME GET THIS STRAIGHT. PCS PHOSPHATE COMPANY WANTS THE taxpayers of North Carolina to build them a sulfur factory at the Morehead City Harbor facility!? Nobody is this stupid, not even the North Carolina Council of State. Something really smells! (Pun intended!)

Where is the NC Department for the Environment and Natural Resources? The Department of Costal Management? Coastal Resources Commission? The Scientific Panel for Coastal Hazards? The Scientific Panel for Energy Development? The UNC, Duke, and all the other schools of marine science? Based upon their own projections, sea level rise will have this plant underwater before completion!!!

Oh, I get it!!! This state-supported enterprise will be a bigger success than the Global TransPark!??

I've got a better idea. Why not build it in Raleigh? The odor would blend with the stench of corruption that already pervades the capital! Imagine how many state jobs would be created!!! Combined with the one-billion-dollar bridge around Pea Island, we could eliminate unemployment in our lifetime!!!

If Raleigh is so intent on making a sow's ear out of silk, here are some more suggestions for Carteret County!

Convert Ft. Macon to a state prison.

Convert Roosevelt National Forest to a landfill. Convert Shackleford Banks to a bombing range. Use the offshore disposal area for nuclear waste. Thanks, Bev, but no thanks!!!

July 19, 2011

# TAXATION BY ANY OTHER NAME

*First proposed in 2011, S.2146 - Clean Energy Standard Act of 2012 was passed by the US Congress the following year. The Renewable Energy Bill required Duke Power in North Carolina to subsidize alternative energy sources such as wind and solar energy.*

---

No POLITICIAN EVER GOT DEFEATED BY UNDERESTIMATING THE ignorance of taxpayers. You take the Renewable Energy Bill. Please!!!

In a nutshell, the Renewable Energy Bill requires Duke Power to pick up the cost of subsidizing wind and solar-energy enterprises, which are already subsidized by Uncle Sam. Although the market value of crude oil is $60/barrel, producing a kilowatt of energy from wind and solar energy costs about $150/barrel. The tax will be disguised as a rate increase in your utility bill long after the politicians have achieved "Dedicated Public Servant" status.

Can't we find a better use for tax dollars? Teachers' salaries? Eliminating the debt of the electric cities? A regional airport for the Global TransPark? Sand transfers to preserve beaches and the tourism and tax dollars they generate? What could we do for the Charlotte Panthers or the Raleigh Hurricanes? Another pay raise for nonessential personnel? Think up your own top-ten list and send it to your representative in Raleigh.

Finally, put on a red nose, join the moral majority, and send a message to the General Assembly: "I'm not a dumb taxpayer! I'm mad as hell and I'm not taking it anymore!!!"

Circa 2011

# THINKING BIG?

*Richard Moore was the North Carolina State Treasurer from 2001–2009. He was first elected to that post in 2000 and re-elected in 2004. The Southport International Seaport was never built.*

---

> *"This (Southport International Seaport (S.I.S.) is thinking big, and it's what we need to do more of."*
> —Richard Moore, Council of State

WITH ALL DUE RESPECT TO THE STATE TREASURER AND THE COUNCIL of State, the best central-economic-planning body in the history of mankind is just recovering from a twelve-year recession. That would be Japan.

In the state's chase to capture the growing distribution and logistics industry, they propose to deepen the Cape Fear River to fifty-two feet. The Council envisions Southport becoming New

Charleston. At these depths, New Orleans would be a better comparison because Oak Island, Wrightsville Beach, Baldhead, Carolina Beach, and Kure Beach will become part of the Atlantic Ocean.

Take a look at the world globe. Look at China. Look at India. Look at the Panama Canal. The Panama Canal is the busiest sea-transport zone in the world. The Canal can only accommodate ships drawing thirty-six feet of water. North Carolina is simply on the wrong side of the world.

Baby boomers from Tennessee to Utah want to retire to water-front communities. Take an aerial view of the coastal plains of North Carolina. What do you see?

Between the Council of State's obsession with cement and mortar, and the Coastal Resources Commission's Retreat from the Shoreline agenda, eastern North Carolinians may never achieve sustainable economic growth.

February 8, 2006

# VOTE CREATION

*The State of North Carolina initiated the development of the North Carolina Maritime Strategy to serve as an open evaluation of North Carolina's position, opportunities and challenges in global maritime commerce. Fortunately, common sense overcame state vanity and the Southport International Seaport never came to fruition.*

---

IF YOU HAVEN'T HAD A CHANCE TO READ THE LATEST N.C. MARITIME Strategy produced by the Dalton/Conti/Perdue brain trust, life expectancy may preclude a complete review. About the length of the King James Bible and as prophetic as a fortune teller's crystal ball, the financial projections would make Enron accountants blush!

Based upon the premise that huge Post Panamax vessels with quadrupled capacity will alter international shipping from Asia and India, the report promises jobs and economic growth—the same jobs and economic growth promised in similar reports from Miami-Dade to New York Harbor. For those of us east of I-95, more jobs and economic growth are promises at least as old as the Global TransPark.

When these vessels will be built, and "how many" is not mentioned in these reports. What appears self-evident is that fewer vessels require fewer ports. Besides, predictions that sea level rise will soon inundate our coastline, North Carolina's lack of natural seaports presents logistical obstacles that can only be paid for with federal earmarks and general obligation bonds. These ships require harbor depths of 50 feet and proportionately larger widths. The environmental damage to seafood and wildlife estuaries is not mentioned in the report—only the costs to dredge and maintain the gargantuan harbors.

With all due respect, if there were a top-ten list of dubious schemes proposed by the Council of State, the Governor's Logistics Task Force, and the NCDOT, this would be number one. When you take into consideration the delicate beauty of eastern North Carolina's coastline, this proposal makes the sulfur factory and windmill schemes appear well conceived.

March 26, 2012

# ARMED AND NON-ESSENTIAL

*From October 1 to October 17, 2013, the United States federal government entered a shutdown and curtailed most routine operations because neither legislation appropriating funds for fiscal year 2014 nor a continuing resolution for the interim authorization of appropriations for fiscal year 2014 was enacted in time. As a result, departments and agencies including the U.S. Fish and Wildlife Service field offices were closed.*

———

IF YOU HAVEN'T VISITED THE OUTER BANKS THIS OCTOBER, DON'T bother. Due to the government shutdown, U.S. Fish and Wildlife (USF&W) troops have orders to thwart public access by North Carolinians attempting to visit the Outer Banks. Drum Fishermen in Buxton were threatened with trespassing if they didn't abandon their catch and get off the island!!!

Now this hardly sounds like life, liberty, and the pursuit of happiness. Sounds more like feudalism when the king not only owned the land but the deer on the land. Besides, *any agent common enough to take your fish would probably cut you!!****

Who owns the Outer Banks? Who owns the Drum in Drum Inlet? If USF&W has orders to thwart public access, should Bogue Banks also close public access until government shutdown is ended? Should these agents be considered nonessential personnel? How much authority does a badge and a gun entitle nonessential personnel?

Not since the fall of Fort Macon have North Carolinians been under such siege by federal forces! Who gave the orders? Are we being occupied because we have Republicans in Raleigh? Why not send the troops to occupy Raleigh along with the political moral majority!!!

What's next? IRS audit? Reconstruction?

*Ready to ride and spread the alarm from Snow Hill.*

October 9, 2013

***ACKNOWLEDGMENT TO BROTHER DAVE GARDNER, REST HIS SOUL. *(A woman common enough to take your dog in a divorce settlement will probably cut you!)*

# ON IMPEACHMENT, CLIMATE CHANGE & POLITICAL CORRECTNESS

*According to the Merriam-Webster dictionary, cancel culture is defined as: the practice or tendency of engaging in mass canceling as a way of expressing disapproval and exerting social pressure. According to Wikipedia, "Cancel culture or call-out culture is a phrase contemporary to the late 2010s and early 2020s used to refer to a form of ostracism in which someone is thrust out of social or professional circles – whether it be online, on social media, or in person."*

---

*"Cancelling cultures is prerequisite to rewriting history. Destroying history is prerequisite to destroying the people."* —George Orwell—*1984*

*"Something momentous happens to a society when they accept an orthodoxy and entrust the interpretation of that orthodoxy to an elite few. They may get to heaven but will never get to the moon. (SIC)"*
—Dr. Daniel Robinson

GIVEN THE REPUGNANT PERSONALITY AND BIZARRE PERSONAL HABITS, Winston Churchill would surely have been impeached on the grounds he was bad and dangerous. Except for scotch and cigars for breakfast, Churchill and Trump's personalities are remarkably similar. Could the congress penchant for bringing impeachment charges and the neo-abolitionist movement hold Thomas Jefferson accountable?

If you asked followers of CNN-ism what is the greatest existential threat to the country, the response would be "climate change." Contrary to Obamanism, the eminent threat to the Republic is the *cancel culture*. What we can watch, hear, or read is controlled by a handful of rich and powerful neo-Marxist oligarchs. In short, critical thinking has been sacrificed on the altar of political correctness.

What would a discourse on climate change between President Obama and Socrates sound like?

**Socrates**: Given the weather events in Texas recently, is this an example of global warming or climate change?

**Obama**: Climate change.

**Socrates**: How do we stop climate change?

**Obama**: By reducing greenhouse gases, especially AGW $CO_2$.

**Socrates**: Expressed in PPM, what level of $CO_2$ do we hope to achieve?

**Obama**: We hope to achieve zero $CO_2$ emissions. We do not know what impact this will have on PPM, but it should lower green-house gases.

**Socrates**: Can we agree the record-cold temperatures impacting 100 million Americans recently are not evidence of global warming?

**Obama**: The entire scientific community supports reducing CO2 emissions to reduce greenhouse gases.

**Socrates**: Without knowing the levels of CO2 that will sustain photosynthesis while reducing greenhouse gases, could we tip the climate into global cooling and the onslaught of an Ice Age? Do we need a contingency plan in case "zero emissions" causes unintended catastrophic consequences? Perhaps bring back the Keystone pipeline?

**Obama**: No. Follow the science.

My apologies to Dr. Robinson and Socrates.

February 18, 2021

# WHICH IS IT?

*Climate variability includes all the variations in the climate that last longer than individual weather events, whereas the term climate change only refers to those variations that persist for a longer period of time, typically decades or more. To illustrate this point, publications dating back to April 1975 were reprinted.*

---

THERE ARE OMINOUS SIGNS THAT THE EARTH'S WEATHER PATTERNS have begun to change dramatically with serious political implications for just about every nation on earth. The evidence in support of these predictions has now begun to accumulate so massively that meteorologists are hard-pressed to keep up with it. Last April, in the most devastating outbreak of tornadoes ever recorded, 148 twisters killed more than 300 people and caused half a billion dollars' worth of damage in thirteen U.S. states.

If the climatic change is as profound as some of the pessimists fear, the resulting famines could be catastrophic. The drop in food output could begin quite soon, perhaps only ten years from now.

To scientists, these incidents represent the advance signs of fundamental change in the world's climate. Climatologists are pessimistic that political leaders will take any positive action to allay effects of climate change, e.g., melting the arctic ice cap.

*"THE CENTRAL FACT IS THAT AFTER THREE QUARTERS OF A CENTURY OF EXTRAORDINARILY MILD CONDITIONS, THE EARTH'S CLIMATE SEEMS TO BE COOLING DOWN."*
   —Newsweek Magazine. April 28, 1975

*"Within the current 800,000-year ice age, there have been warmer and colder times, called "interglacial" and "glacial" periods. This is caused by periodic changes in three things: Earth's orbit around the sun, the tilt of Earth's axis, and the wobble of the Earth around its axis."*
   —February 4, 2020, Paleontological Society.

*"Antarctic sea ice is frozen seawater topped by frozen snow. In the Antarctic, sea ice circles the continent and covers a large area. Since the late 1970s, the Antarctic has gained an average of 7,300 square miles (18,900 sq km) of sea ice per year, peaking in 2014."*
   —NASA Global Climate Change

June 7, 2021

# CHAPTER V

## HAPPY JACK®, THE WRIGHT BROTHERS & BIG BUSINESS

# HAPPY JACK®, INC.

When de Tocqueville visited the United States in the nineteenth century, he remarked, *"...what most astonished me in the United States was not so much the grandeur of some undertakings as the innumerable multitude of small ones."*

---

As FAR BACK AS I CAN REMEMBER, THANKSGIVING DINNERS HAD always been late at my house. Thanksgiving had a special significance: it marked the opening day of hunting season and a late chase would inevitably keep us from the traditional family meal. It didn't seem to matter, though, because hounds and hunting were as much a part of Thanksgiving to the Exums as turkey and cranberry sauce.

That's probably why it succeeded. The idea to start a business that was a hobby.

Based upon traditional business principles, the business should have failed miserably. The company's financial backing, what there was of it, did not come from stockholders or banks, but from the stud fees generated by an old field champion— Contentnea Jack—and at the age of 12, old Jack couldn't hold out forever. For production facilities, a 1936 Maytag washing machine sufficed for mixing Jim Exum's ingenious sarcoptic mange formula. The organizational chart didn't look like much either. There were Jim and Mary Exum (management) and Leslie and Lena Grant (production), and, on busy days, those lines became obscured.

But it survived. Mother, Daddy, Lena, Leslie, and old Jack are all gone, the EPA made us get rid of the 1936 Maytag washing machine, and Thanksgiving hunts gave way to ever increasing business demands…

## THE AGE OF REGULATION IS BORN

THE UNITED STATES ENVIRONMENTAL PROTECTION AGENCY (EPA) was created in 1970 by President Richard Nixon. The EPA was created with the goal to ensure clean air and water and "protect human health and the environment." In 1973, Happy Jack® received the following chilling notification from a bureaucrat in the newly created Environmental Protection Agency:

> *A review of our files indicates that there is no data to support the effectiveness of this product. All previous information that you have submitted are only testimonials and are unacceptable. Moreover, we have serious reservations about the safety of this product. Namely the use of turpentine on raw or broken skin. This is to notify you that in accordance with Section 6(b) of the FIFRA Act as amended (86 STAT. 984) the registration of this product will be cancelled effective 30 days after receipt of this letter.*

The next three years brought the reality of bureaucratic nightmare to Snow Hill as the fate of our small business hung in the balance. This is where all the essays began.

*The Raleigh News & Observer* rejected the Wright Brothers editorial as "not being newsworthy." However, as a second thought, a carbon copy of the editorial was sent to *The Washington Post*, where it was published and incorporated into Senator Helms' monthly newsletter by one of his staff members. A relative in Fayetteville, North Carolina, saw the letter in Helms' monthly newsletter and mailed it to me. From despair to elation, I was determined to syndicate myself. Prior to syndication, however, we were in a race against time in satisfying the brand-new bureaucrat and his concerns about turpentine. Our senators and congressman were very sympathetic, but they acknowledged that they could not help us. In fact, the regulators served as judge, jury, and executioner unless they were challenged in the courts. The first order of business was to find some mangy dogs to prove our mange remedy was effective and safe, even though our mange remedy had been in interstate commerce for thirty years with a money-back guarantee.

The red tape thickened when we were told to develop a protocol, and for this, we needed an attorney to act as a liaison between the EPA and Happy Jack®. We were running up bills that rivaled the federal deficit without a protocol or how it would be performed.

Our local veterinarian reluctantly agreed to conduct the tests if we could find some mangy dogs to conduct the tests. The local animal shelter was reluctant to submit inmates to tests where safety might be an issue. When asked the prognosis for these unwanted animals, the shelter manager acknowledged they would be euthanized. Twelve mangy dogs and two months of treatment produced twelve adoptable animals and a 100% safe and effective result.

Without the help of a sympathetic Washington, D.C., Russian immigrant attorney, none of this would have happened. But that's another story.

# THE WRIGHT BROTHERS' STORY

*The Occupational Safety and Health Administration (OSHA) was founded in 1971 by President Richard Nixon. OSHA is a federal agency that focuses on analyzing and reducing occupational hazards in the workplace by providing education and training, as well as by enforcing federal regulations and standards. OSHA became small business' biggest nightmare. OSHA's OIG folks are armed. They are GS series 1811 law enforcement officers, and as such, they enforce criminal provisions of US Code.*

*In 1975, Bill Barlow, owner of an electrical and plumbing installation business in Pocatello, Idaho, who was continually harassed by armed agents at his machine shop without a warrant, sued OSHA for "unreasonable search & seizure." Barlow was victorious, giving small business the same rights as individuals.*

*The Democratic-appointed N.C. Attorney General filed an amicus curiae brief on behalf of OSHA. Critics site statistics that question cost/benefit of OSHA over the 50 years of existence.*

RECENTLY THE AEROMOBILE, THE AUTOMOBILE THAT FLIES, HAS BEEN grounded by a myriad of federal agencies because, among other things, the aeromobile does not meet bumper standards. The thought occurred to this observer, suppose we had been blessed with these agencies earlier in the Republic's history, say 1900. The news might have sounded like this…

"Today, Occupational Safety & Health agents closed the Wright Brothers' Bicycle Shop and levied a stiff fine for failing to comply with safety regulations regarding placement of ladders and exactly whether Orville Wright's grease pit constituted a hole as defined by OSHA regulation 12-A, Section 3 (c) (1) (d), paragraph 3. Orville explained he was trying to build a flying machine heavier than air and was unfamiliar with the regulation. Whereupon the agent asked if they had applied for an Environmental Protection Agency establishment number. Wilbur Wright, Orville's brother, answered, 'No, but if it will help us get our machine in the air, we'll make application.'

"Application was denied by the Chief Administrator stating: 'This onerous contraption poses not only unreasonable adverse effects to the environment but an imminent hazard to the public. Besides,' the Chief Administrator added, 'if the Good Lord meant for us to fly, he would have put wings on our back.'"

"In other news, the President seemed baffled by a slowing economy…"

Published in *The Washington Post*, 1976

# GUESS WHAT, DUMB
# CONSUMER???

*The United States Consumer Products Safety Commission (CPSC) was created by Congress in its Consumer Product Safety Act. The CPSC is an independent federal agency that develops and maintains standards for consumer products (such as lawn mowers, toys for children, etc.) with the goal of reducing the risk of harm to consumers. The CPSC is also responsible for researching products that have the potential to cause harm to consumers and secures recalls of faulty products if needed. There are no sunset laws for regulatory agencies and justifying existence requires increasingly creative thinkers at the Chief Administrator level. Ralph Nader epitomized the corporate watch dog and is known for his book,* Unsafe at Any Speed.

---

GUESS WHAT? THE PRICE OF LAWNMOWERS IS GOING UP. THANKS TO the latest kid on the bureaucratic block: The Consumer Products Safety Commission. Although overshadowed by the banality of sister organizations such as FDA, headed by Donald "Duck" (as in

"Look Out") Kennedy and OSHA, (America's answer to the Third Reich), the CPSC is beginning to make significant contribution to the bureaucratic dribble (and hence the cost of living) coming out of Washington.

I first became aware of CPSC this past summer when the local radio station blared a warning against snow skiing because many people had their legs broken while snow skiing. (Don't worry Aspen, there aren't that many snow skiers in Snow Hill, especially in July!)

More recently, the CPSC has gotten downright dictatorial in their edicts. After an exten$ive study, they issued the following decree on the rotary lawn mower:

1. Do not place hands and feet under mower while running.
2. Do not pour gas on hot engine block.
3. If you must put hands and feet under power mower while running, run engine slowly to minimize mutilation.

(BY THE WAY, FOR THOSE INTERESTED, THERE ARE THREE JOB OPENINGS at CPSC testing lab.)

That's not all!!! Last week CPSC determined through controlled studies by recognized experts, "the tricycle is unsafe at any speed." Moreover, the CPSC is presently undertaking a study to determine the lethal nature of the grocery cart!!!! Enough you say!!! A Naderistic Tool you say!!!! Think again, dumb consumer!!! Next year Ted Kennedy will try to add yet another goofy group: The National Health Insurance Agency. (Ted thinks Proposition 13 is a proposal of marriage.) And you can bet you could get cheaper "insurance" from the Mafia.

January 16, 1979

# PSYCHIC JOINS SMALL BUSINESS ENDANGERED SPECIES LIST

*Psychics are individuals who claim to possess a variety of seemingly unexplainable abilities, such as clairvoyance. Historically, psychics have often been looked down upon and viewed with skepticism in Western society. However, in recent years, the general population has become less skeptical about psychics and their abilities.*

---

IN THE TRUE SPIRIT OF INDEPENDENCE DAY, THE WAYNE COUNTY Commissioners (Goldsboro, N.C.) have chosen to put psychics on the small-business endangered-species list. Psychics will join a long list of politically incorrect businesses threatened by the Clintonistas including tobacco, logging, and pharmaceutical among others. To ensure Mom & Pop fortune-telling businesses don't get off the ground, a prominent politician and attorney (that's not an oxymoron, or is it?) will bring the full force and authority of the N.C. General Assembly to bear on this next- to-oldest profession— all because "There's no scientific evidence that palm reading really works."

Suppose this same criterion were applied to the County Commissioners and General Assembly, not to mention the Congress? Some folks can't remember when these august bodies ever did work!

Will this decree include Merrill Lynch that employs over 10,000 psychics nationwide? History is replete with psychics! What kind of reception would John the Baptist get in Wayne County today!

Besides, if they keep eliminating small businesses, who's going to keep attorneys and politicians in the style of living to which they have become accustomed? Pretty soon, TV evangelism will be the only way to make an honest buck! And they don't pay taxes! At the risk of lawyer bashing, why don't the county commissioners consider the legal and political professions for elimination? Think of the money that would be saved and the mental anguish eliminated! The campaign song could begin as follows:

*"Mamas, don't let your children grow up,*
    *to be lawyers, politicians, and such!"*
—Paraphrased from Waylon Jennings and Willie Nelson

MERRILL LYNCH BROKERS FROM WINSTON-SALEM TO WILSON, NORTH Carolina, responded acknowledging empathy *and* sympathy for fortune tellers.

July 1, 1994

# CHAPTER VI

## FRIENDS OF MAN'S BEST FRIEND &
## THE LOVE OF DOGS

### CREATION'S SOUL

It may be heresy to associate spiritual journeys with the animals we have loved. On the other hand, those relationships are as close to unconditional love as we may experience in our spiritual journeys. Like rings on a tree, my life can be chronicled by the dogs I have loved.

# BUSTER BROWN (1995–2009)

*"If I could but give to my walk of life the same loyal kindness of a master's hound, then I would have been a better man than seldom is ever found."*
—Jim Exum Sr., Founder Happy Jack®, Inc.

Unwanted and abused animals are a tragedy of biblical proportion. The experience of a visit to the animal shelter is truly unforgettable. The animals do their best to be noticed in hopes you will pick them from all the rest. They are literally on death row through no fault of their own. In 2006, we considered funding an animal hospital dedicated to spay/neuter as well as a mobile clinic. Both ideas were beyond *Happy Jack®'s* ability to fund such an undertaking. We decided that the most cost-effective approach would be to subsidize the cost of spay/neuter procedures. We established the 501(3)(c) *Friends of Man's Best Friend*, to sell spay/neuter certificates for $25/each and redeem them for $75/each. The response was overwhelming as an army of rescue organizations emerged east of Interstate 95 and the number of spay/neuter procedures skyrocketed from less than 20 to over

2,000 a year. Our ability to raise funds to meet our $50 subsidy was far exceeded by the demand for the certificates. *Happy Jack®* made up the difference. We are solving this problem in eastern North Carolina with a legion of rescue groups purchasing, and animal clinics accepting, our subsidized spay/neuter vouchers. This is our history.

| Year | 2009 | 2015 | 2016 | 2017 | 2018 | 2019 | 2020 | 2021 |
|---|---|---|---|---|---|---|---|---|
| Dogs Admitted | 2036 | 1177 | 1251 | 1153 | 1092 | 811 | 791 | 699 |
| Euthanized | 763 | 309 | 335 | 183 | 82 | 52 | 36 | 17 |
| Cats Admitted | 1580 | 1097 | 1088 | 972 | 857 | 732 | 740 | 635 |
| Euthanized | 634 | 481 | 392 | 188 | 132 | 119 | 40 | 1 |

*WHILE THERE ARE NO LEASH LAWS FOR DOGS STATE-WIDE IN NORTH Carolina, certain counties within North Carolina do have leash laws, which require dogs to be on a leash in public. Buster was grandfathered by the author exempting him from the new leash laws, having arrived in Pine Knoll Shores years before the leash law bureaucrats at town hall.*

*THIS EDITORIAL WAS REALLY BUSTER'S HOMILY AND WHEN IT WAS penned, I kept telling myself the joy of having him outweighed the sorrow of losing him. Obviously, the essay touched the hearts of the Pine Knoll Shores police when I received calls asking if Buster had been found.*

## BUSTER BROWN (1995–2009)

I keep hoping that the phone will ring, and the voice on the other end will say, *"We've got Buster."* Buster had a lot of friends.

In the 14 years we jogged Bogue Banks, we saw a lot of changes: the debauched Iron Steamer Pier, public access dug into the barrier dunes without regard to turtle estuaries or the delicate ecological balance. Buster never showed much deference for the

Raleigh Brain Trust and his contempt for the N.C. Ports Authority and the Army Corps of Engineers was evident when the beach seemed to disappear under our very feet after the 1993 gouging of Beaufort Inlet.

Perhaps the biggest change in Buster's life was the introduction of what he viewed as the Leash Nazi. He was baffled why his two-legged relatives at PKS Town Hall would pay a grown man to harass oceanfront taxpayers by swooping down on unsuspecting victims without leashes. To be sure, this person could do something constructive: plant sea oats, pick up trash, or guard the turtles.

Buster never held a grudge against PKS Town Hall or the uncivil servants who dreamed up such barbaric regulations. He had great fun outrunning and outwitting the Leash Nazi until he was too old to get out of the way. Even then, he defied the inhumanity of the leash.

I still go to our favorite places: Trinity Center, the old Ramada Inn. My heart jumps when, out of nowhere, the Leash Nazi swoops down with his ATV armed with the latest taser technology hoping that he'll catch Buster off leash.

He's not at our favorite places anymore. The phone call won't come. The hole in my heart tells me that Buster's not coming home. He was my best friend.

June 9, 2009

# CREATION'S SOUL

*The following editorial was directed at Wake County and all the Wake Counties that tolerate the gruesome statistics of unwanted and abandoned creatures.*

———

HAVE YOU EVER BEEN TO AN ANIMAL SHELTER AND WATCHED THE abandoned creatures on death row? They have done nothing wrong and are there through no fault of their own. They are instinctively aware of the power you hold and will perform their best "pick-me" routine in hopes that you will rescue them from their gruesome fate. Not even Barry Saunders (N&O columnist) can bring humor to the killings in Wake County where the technology of slaughter can only accommodate 50 animals per day, 365 days per year. These are the animals that so desperately want to live.

This tragic and complex problem can be solved by charging a fee for unneutered pets and effecting spay/neuter procedures with the proceeds. According to *The Week Magazine: "The number of pets euthanized in the U.S. has plummeted from some 20 million in 1970 to about 3 million last year … The biggest reason for the change is widespread acceptance of neutering."* All too often, the hope for this solution ends at the professional politician's office door.

A voucher program is a similar solution funded differently. *Friends of Man's Best Friend* sells $75 spay/neuter payment vouchers to consumers for $25.00. When the voucher is presented at a clinic, *Friends of Man's Best Friend* reimburses the clinic $75 against the total spay/neuter costs. The former receives funds from local donors, an annually sponsored golf tournament, and *Happy Jack®* to provide additional funds when donations are not enough. *Friends of Man's Best Friend* celebrated its eighteenth anniversary in May 2022.

*Lord of all creatures, we offer this prayer —*
*For the one-eyed, lop-eared, three-legged lame,*
*The worm-eaten, slab-sided, bare of hair,*
*For the worn and cast out, wild or tame,*
*The unbright, unsightly, toothless, knock-kneed,*
*Stiff-jointed, gray-muzzled old, deaf or blind,*
*For the slack-jawed, splay-footed, worst of breed,*
*Used up and abused by man unkind,*
*For the sick and starving that patiently wait*
*Without whine or whimper to suffer their fate —*
*Because they all share Creation's soul,*
*In your kingdom, Lord, make them lovely and whole!*
—Janet Adkins (1983)

Wake County should be ashamed. We all should be ashamed.
Joe Exum, Sr., Executive Director
*Friends of Man's Best Friend*

. . .

IT MAY BE HERESY TO ASSOCIATE SPIRITUAL JOURNEYS WITH THE animals we have loved. On the other hand, those relationships are as close to unconditional love as we may experience in our spiritual journeys. Like rings on a tree, my life can be chronicled by the dogs I have loved. This editorial was really Buster's homily and when it was penned, I kept telling myself the joy of loving him outweighed the sorrow of losing him. Obviously, the essay touched the hearts of the Pine Knoll Shores police when I received calls asking if Buster had been found.

December 9, 2012

# AN APOLOGY TO MAN'S BEST FRIEND

*In Pine Knoll Shores, North Carolina, there is an ordinance that requires dog owners to clean up and properly dispose of pet waste. However, in recent years, residents have continued to hold town hall meetings related to the issues: often along Mason-Dixon lines.*

WITNESSING PINE KNOLL SHORE'S INCORPORATION AND THE BUDGET necessary to sustain town hall has been a subject for editorial comment. My apologies if Buster and I have a special perspective on this development.

————

*"Dog waste is a threat to the health of our children, degrades our town, and transmits disease."*
    —Pine Knoll Shores, Town Hall

*"The one absolutely unselfish friend that a man can have in this selfish world, the one that never deserts him, and the one that never proves ungrateful or treacherous, is his dog."*
    —Senator Vest's tribute to the dog

ON A SCALE OF 1 TO 10, I SUSPECT DOG WASTE IS RIGHT UP THERE with turtle poop, seagull splatter, and baby pool urine as a health threat to our children. From a sleepy, little community nestled in the Roosevelt Maritime Forest, Pine Knoll Shores has finally become Atlantic Beach, teeming with property flippers, obsessive compulsive germophobes, and three fulltime police persons on ATVs trying to snatch any unsuspecting, unleashed, four-legged creature from their owner's front yard. Further degradation to the township at this point would seem a remote possibility.

*"Heaven is by favor: if it were by merit, your dog would go in and you would stay out."*
    —Mark Twain

Hopefully, Mark Twain was just a babbling old fool. Otherwise, Pine Knoll Shores Town Hall may need some help at the Pearly Gates!

June 28, 2006

# LEG LIMITATIONS

*Though few states have state-wide leash laws, most states do have some version of leash laws in at least a handful of municipalities. Each leash law varies depending on the area, but generally, leash laws require pets remain on a leash in public places. Similarly, laws that limit the amount of time a dog can be tethered to a post, tree, etc., also commonly accompany such leash laws.*

THERE ARE HUGE CULTURAL DIFFERENCES FOR THOSE WHO ESCAPE New Jersey for the culture of North Carolina especially when it comes to dogs. Leash laws are the first priority in an effort to create the environment from which they escaped. Cary has come a long way since it was best known as a speed trap by UNC students between Chapel Hill and St. Mary's.

---

WHAT DO CARY AND SAN FRANCISCO HAVE IN COMMON? NOT MUCH apparently, especially when it comes to how we treat our best friends.

The Cary Town Council wants to limit every household to just two best friends. In San Francisco, the people want to abolish leash laws. The thinking among Californians is understandable: Put leashes on four-legged Californians today, it's just a matter of time before they put leashes on two-legged Californians.

Cary is in a different situation entirely. Limitations on household creatures have been placed on the wrong species. Until immigration laws can be strengthened, households pronouncing Cary as *Kah-ree* should be limited to a maximum of seven legs (mix or match). People who talk funny and exceed the seven-leg limit would be exported immediately to wherever the hell they came from.

This may seem a little harsh to the P.C. crowd, but it could have been worse. Be glad the Arapahoe and Cherokee didn't think of this before they were pushed off their land. We might all be stuck on the Kahree Reservation!

March 27, 2001

# CORPORATE VS. SMALL BUSINESS STRUCTURE

There are many differences in the corporate structure and the structure of a small business. Primarily, there are no job descriptions. When people ask me what I do at Happy Jack®, I respond, "What do you want me to do?" I cannot recall what I was doing when this letter arrived in the mail, but the response would require undivided attention.

---

*January 7, 1982*

*Dear Happy Jack®,*

*I want a horse but I didn't ask my mom yet because I don't know what to say. Can you help me? Following are the things I must know:*

*How to ask her?*
*When to ask her?*
*What to say?*

*Please answer these! I am nine years old, but I'll be ten in April. I know a lot about horses, like NOT to water them after a long run, and if you have a lock on the stable, have a good one, because the horses will chew on it and learn the combination and unlock it. I've read a lot in books about them and know a lot. I know where to keep it and what to do to make money. I hope you can help me.*

*Here's my address:*

*Miss Sarah J Syracuse, New York*

*And I say again, I hope you can help me!*

*Signed,*

*Sarah J. ( with a sketch of horse)*

---

*Dear Sarah,*

*We have read your letter with great interest and sincerely hope that we can help.*

*You will be glad to know that my brother and I have a boy and girl just about your age. In fact, Ann wanted a horse for Christmas also. However, there was no place for her to keep the horse and she decided to wait another year. The best time to approach mommas is a difficult question. It is our opinion that mealtime is probably not a good time to ask about the horse. Perhaps bedtime is the best time to talk to your mom. We believe the best way to ask is to tell your mom exactly what you have in mind. Tell her exactly what you told us: how much you know about horses, and how you plan to help with expenses.*

*Taking care of an animal, especially a horse, requires a lot of love, and, not to mention, money. One thing about mommas is that they understand a lot more than we know!*

*We hope you won't mind, but we are sending copies of your letter to the editors of Western Horseman and the* Syracuse Post-Standard. *They are real experts. Call us at no charge at 1-800- 334-8350 to let us know what happens. We will wait for your call.*

*Very truly yours,*

*Happy Jack®, Inc.*
*Joe Exum, Sr.*
*Vice-President*

---

*"Something is happening in our country.... We aren't producing leaders like we used to. A new chief executive officer today, exhausted by the climb to the peak, falls down on the mountaintop and goes to sleep.... I'm afraid leadership is becoming a lost art."*
  — Robert Townsend, Up the Organization (1968)

THE CULTURE IN A SMALL BUSINESS IS MUCH DIFFERENT FROM A corporate culture. The margin for error is smaller—the banks are not lining up to bail you out and earning a profit is not only exhilarating but also essential. When I first saw this message, I envisioned Harry and some Madison Avenue whiz kid coming up with what must have cost employees and stockholders about $50,000. I cannot locate my first correspondence with Harry, but he must have thought that I was enamored with his full-page memos because he sent me a reprint I still have.

. . .

MY APOLOGIES TO MR. GRAY WHEREVER HE MAY BE TODAY, BUT MY disdain for "big business" was second only to Robert Townsend's. Somehow, Mr. Gray's pithy memos touched that nerve and, well, the devil made me do it. The following full-page ad appeared in the *Wall Street Journal* in 1984 under the heading:

### LET'S GET RID OF MANAGEMENT

*People don't want to be managed. They want to be led. Whoever heard of a world manager? World leader, yes. Educational Leader. Political leader. Religious leader. Scout leader. Community leader. Labor leader. Business leader. They lead. They don't manage. The carrot always wins over the stick. Ask your horse. You can lead your horse to water, but you can't manage him to drink. If you want to manage somebody, manage yourself. Do that well and you'll be ready to stop managing, and start leading.*

*—Harry Gray, United Technology CEO,*
*The Wall Street Journal*

---

*April 12, 1984*

*Dear Harry,*

*I don't know what you're smoking, but if you would enclose a little with the 8½ by 11 reprint, I sure would appreciate it. I asked my horse about the carrot and stick. Ethel and the children overheard our conversation and said I should take a few days off. I told them I was managing myself. Joe, Jr. said I'd get pimples. What if I lead myself?*

*Your friend,*

*Joe Exum, Sr., Vice President, Happy Jack®, Inc.*

*Cc: The Wall Street Journal*

———

APPARENTLY, HARRY WAS NOT DISSUADED BY MY MEMOS.

———

*December 18, 1984*

*Dear Harry,*

*In the past, perhaps I have been too obtuse in my comments on your "messages" in the* Wall Street Journal. *I will be more direct. Harry, someone should update us from time to time on Paine's* Common Sense.

*But Harry, it shouldn't be you. You're giving capitalism a bad name! You make the post office look efficient. Besides, when Paine wrote Common Sense, there were no gas tanks for Chrissake! And Harry, whatever you do, don't compound this silly allocation of resources by sending me a reprint. I know I've hurt your feelings but it's for your own good. Nobody wants to be known as the Jim Jones of free enterprise!*

*Your Friend,*

*Joe Exum, Sr., Vice President, Happy Jack®, Inc.*

*P.S. Congratulations on beating the bugging rap!*

———

THEY MADE A BOOK OUT OF HARRY'S MESSAGES!!! I GUESS HE DIDN'T put his pants on one leg at a time. From an entrepreneur's perspective, that attribute should have gone to Robert Townsend.

# MILLIE BUSH'S PUPS

*President George H. W. Bush and First Lady Barbara Bush owned an English Springer Spaniel named Millie, who they brought with them to the White House after President Bush was inaugurated in 1989. Shortly thereafter, Millie had a litter of pups.*

---

SOMETHING HAPPENS TO PEOPLE WHEN THEY REACH THEIR LEVEL OF incompetence. They not only become incompetent but also lose all sense of perspective and, subsequently, their sense of humor. Perhaps one of the most memorable events in Happy Jack®'s history was receiving an order for collars from the Barbara Bush White House after Millie delivered eight pups in 1989. The event caused quite a stir at Happy Jack®, so we called Peggy, editor of the local newspaper. She came out to our plant with a pencil and a camera in hand and put the story on the front page of the Snow Hill *Standard Laconic*.

We were elated and sent the front-page article to the White House knowing that they would be very appreciative since they were all Republicans and everybody in Snow Hill were all Democrats. Not so fast, *yellow dog democrats*!!!

---

*From: The White House, Washington*
*November 29, 1989*

*Dear Mr. Exum,*

*Your recent letter to Linda C., in which you enclosed a copy of a recent article on your sale of "Happy Jack®" collars to the President, has been referred to me for reply.*

*You may not have been aware of it, but the President has a longstanding policy of declining requests to use his name or likeness in connection with commercial activities.*

*His policy applies not only to commercial promotions directly involving the President or the White House but also to the indirect association of the president with a commercial enterprise, even where it is true that the president enjoys the product or service.*

*I am sure that you will understand the need for such a policy. We would appreciate it if, in the future, Happy Jack® would assist us by observing this policy.*

*Thank you for writing and for your kind words of support for President Bush.*

*Sincerely yours,*
*Jay B.*
*Associate counsel to the President*

*Cc: Linda C.*

---

Apparently, Linda was not qualified to handle such intricate matters or perhaps Jay was having a slow day. Nonetheless, I returned his letter with the following note at the bottom.

---

*Dear Mr. B.,*

*I called up Peggy down at the STANDARD LACONIC and told her what you said. I thought maybe she could print a retraction or something. She said you were just an ill-mannered Republican, to send her $10,000 and she would call it a paid political announcement. What do you think? Do I need to get a lawyer?*
*Help,*
*Joe Exum, Sr., Vice President, Happy Jack®, Inc.*

---

I'm not making this up. Something happens to people when they reach their level of incompetence. They not only become incompetent but also lose all sense of perspective and, subsequently, their sense of humor.

I received a phone call from Jay apologizing for any misunderstanding he may have created and reassured me I would not need to have my attorney get involved. (As though I had one!) I thanked him for his call and told him not to worry, it wouldn't happen again.

# EPILOGUE

According to *Letters to the Editor,* motives for *regular letter-writers are the least understood within professional journalism.* Perhaps "The devil made me do it" is the best explanation acknowledging "we are often wrong, but never in doubt."

The history of letters to the editor is a rich one marred by the Sedition Act of 1798 used to silence newspapers sympathetic to Thomas Jefferson as well as suppress voting. Thomas Paine's *Common Sense* and Hamilton's *Federalist* papers were "letters to the editor." Ironically, the Wright Brothers editorial in *Divided States of America* was written in 1976, 200 years after the Declaration of Independence. What the local Raleigh paper rejected as irrelevant, *The Washington Post* chose to publish.

*Divided States of America* has been published not to rub salt in our wounds of division but to highlight events that brought us to this point. We are not divided by accident but by political purpose and listen to anyone in television, academia, social media, or the Internet that validates our opinion. Editorials by nature are meant to be persuasive and provoke critical thinking. Hopefully, these editorials demonstrate a modicum of critical thought and therefore elements of truth if only for baby boomers and our children.

# REFERENCES

*Unless otherwise noted, the information provided in the background section of each section is sourced from Wikipedia.*

**Prologue**

Simon, William E. *A Time for Truth,* Publisher: Penguin Publishing Group (April 1979).

Tse-Tung, Mao. *Quotations from Chairman Mao Tse-Tung (Little Red Book),* Publisher: Foreign Languages Press (1966).

**CHAPTER I**
**Happy Birthday, Dr. King**

https://www.nytimes.com/2018/09/20/us/politics/anita-hill-testimony-clarence-thomas.html

**The Central Planners**

https://www.thebalance.com/us-debt-by-president-by-dollar-and-percent-3306296

Patrick Henry quote: https://www.goodreads.com/quotes/26864-is-life-so-dear-or-peace-so-sweet-as-to

**The Obama Legacy**

2016 Election Results: https://www.archives.gov/electoral-college/2016

https://www.nationalreview.com/2008/09/what-did-obama-do-community-organizer-byron-york/

Alinsky, Saul. *Rules for Radicals: A Pragmatic Primer for Realistic Radicals*, Publisher: Vintage (June 22, 2010).

**Such Men Are Dangerous**

Paine, Thomas. *The American Crisis.*

**Hate Politics**

https://www.history.com/this-day-in-history/james-hodgkinson-shooting-republicans-baseball-game

https://www.history.com/topics/reconstruction/ku-klux-klan

https://www.nytimes.com/2017/08/12/us/charlottesville-protest-white-nationalist.html

**Richmond Falls to WOKE Yankees**

https://www.smithsonianmag.com/smart-news/richmond-confederate-monuments-headed-to-black-history-museum-180979319/

## Radicalized Political Candidates

http://www.crossroad.to/Quotes/communism/alinsky.htm

https://www.the-dispatch.com/story/opinion/letters/2020/03/25/letter-remember-reagans-words-during-this-crisis/41789039/

https://www.ontheissues.org/Archive/Think_Stupid_Ronald_Reagan.htm

## CHAPTER II

### Reparations

https://oag.ca.gov/ab3121/reports

### City of Wokes

https://www.newsobserver.com/sports/article258203313.html#storylink=cpy

### In Defense of Sam

https://dailycaller.com/2022/07/18/university-announces-diversity-initiatives-caving-1619-project-creators-lawsuit/

### Due Process Be Damned

Daugherty, Steve. *Experiments in Honesty: Meditations on Love, Fear and the Honest to God Naked Truth,* Publisher: Worthy Books (March 6, 2018)

### Neo-Civil Rights

https://www.theguardian.com/film/2016/feb/29/al-sharpton-this-will-be-the-last-night-of-an-all-white-oscars

### CHAPTER III

Fake News: https://oed.com/view/Entry/67776#eid1264306660

### Due Process

https://www.politico.com/news/2021/01/29/fbi-lawyer-trump-russia-probe-email-463750

### Bashing China, Part 1

https://www.npr.org/2012/02/07/146466331/chinese-labor-practices-sour-apple-consumers

https://www.npr.org/2012/03/29/149617086/headed-for-the-butcher-chinese-dogs-are-rescued

### "Hoodoo Economics" Clintonomics

https://www.lexico.com/en/definition/voodoo_economics

### CHAPTER IV

### Big-Time Academics

https://www.google.com/url?sa=t&rct=j&q=&esrc=s&source=web&cd=&ved=2ahUKEwi4h8Xbt5X5AhVOEVkFHcqmC88QFnoECAQQAQ&url=https%3A%2F%2Fresearch.collegeboard.org%

2Fmedia%2Fpdf%2Ftrends-college-pricing-2011-full-report.pdf&
usg=AOvVaw2xksrNJC5yzis3GZepXACr

https://www.google.com/url?sa=t&rct=j&q=&esrc=s&source=
web&cd=&ved=2ahUKEwjt3ZiHuZX5AhWSGVkFHYmKB6UQF
noECAMQAw&url=https%3A%2F%2Fstudentservices.ncsu.edu%
2Fforms%2Fcashier%2Ftuition-archives%2FFall_2011_archive.
pdf&usg=AOvVaw3owGHe1acD1klXkeRBx3l5

**Dook's Roots**

https://perfect-free.typepad.com/the-perfect-and-the-free/2011/
11/can-tuition-keep-rising.html

https://library.duke.edu/rubenstein/uarchives/history/articles/
statistics

https://www.google.com/url?sa=t&rct=j&q=&esrc=s&source=
web&cd=&cad=rja&uact=8&ved=2ahUKEwi-qJf6uZX5Ah
WQD1kFHbxMCqsQFnoECAgQAw&url=https%3A%2F%2Fto
day.duke.edu%2F2022%2F02%2Ftrustees-meet-approve-tuition-
and-fees-2022-23&usg=AOvVaw3DYp3rBRD1n_44xMbKoLQm

**To Seem Rather Than to Be**

https://www.google.com/url?sa=t&rct=j&q=&esrc=s&source=
web&cd=&cad=rja&uact=8&ved=2ahUKEwjSuJmwupX5Ah
WMGVkFHQ-PA14QFnoECBAQAw&url=https%3A%2F%
2Fwww.ncpedia.org%2Fesse-quam-videri&usg=
AOvVaw30w6vCoU8UzSCJW0SMQgo4

https://www.espn.com/college-football/story/_/id/6809612/
butch-davis-fired-north-carolina-football-coach

## Some Things Are Priceless

https://www.nytimes.com/2013/07/10/opinion/the-decline-of-north-carolina.html

## Dredged Material Mismanagement Plan

https://www.carteretcountync.gov/639/Dredged-Material-Management-Plan-DMMP

Pilkey, Orrin H. *How to live with an island: A handbook to Bogue Banks, North Carolina,* Publisher:  North Carolina Dept. of Natural and Economic Resources (January 1, 1975).

## Being Green

https://www.southernenvironment.org/press-release/epa-determination-of-unacceptable-environmental-harm-triggers-examination-o/

https://www.quoteauthors.com/thomas-jefferson-quotes/

https://www.goodreads.com/quotes/92283-government-s-view-of-the-economy-could-be-summed-up-in

## The Misery Index

https://www.cfr.org/backgrounder/opec-changing-world

## Converting Silk to a Sow's Ear!!!

https://www.carolinacoastonline.com/news_times/news/article_6c851a4a-4008-5107-811b-5ed16ee2e594.html

## Taxation by Any Other Name

https://news.duke-energy.com/releases/duke-energy-reaches-deal-with-renewable-organizations-to-modernize-rooftop-solar-policy-in-north-carolina

## CHAPTER V

## Happy Jack®, Inc.

Happy Jack® is a trademark of HAPPY JACK, INC.

## The Wright Brothers' Story

https://uswtmc.org/news/osha-warrantless-inspections-marshall-v-barlows-inc

## CHAPTER VI

## Creation's Soul

https://www.kinston.com/story/opinion/editorials/2012/12/09/letters-to-editor-for-sunday/34337771007/

ADDENDUM

THE WHITE HOUSE
WASHINGTON

November 29, 1989

Dear Mr. Exum:

Your recent letter to Linda C, in which you enclosed a copy
of a recent article on your sale of "Happy Jack" collars to the
President, has been referred to me for reply.

You may not have been aware of it, but the President has a longstanding policy of declining requests to use his name or likeness
in connection with commercial activities. His policy applies not
only to commercial promotions directly involving the President or
the White House, but also to the indirect association of the
President with a commercial product or service, even where it is
true that the President enjoys the product or service.

I am sure that you will understand the need for such a policy.
We would appreciate it if, in the future, Happy Jack would assist
us by observing this policy.

Thank you for writing and for your kind words of support for
President Bush.

Mr. Joe Exum
Happy Jack, Inc.
P.O. Box 475 Highway 258 South
Snow Hill, North Carolina 28580

cc:  Linda C.

Dear Mr. B ,

I called up Peggy down at the STANDARD LACONIC and told her what
you said.  I thought maybe she could print a retraction or something.
She said you were just an ill-bred Republican, to send her $10,000
and she would call it a paid political announcement.  What do you
think?  Do I need to get a lawyer.

Help,

Joe Exum    cc:  Linda C

*Letter from the White House - Millie Bush's Pups*

**The News and Observer** ▲ **THE RALEIGH TIMES**

MORNING AND SUNDAY
SERVING EASTERN NORTH CAROLINA AND THE RESEARCH TRIANGLE

AFTERNOON
COVERING THE CAPITAL AREA

215 SOUTH McDOWELL STREET • RALEIGH, NORTH CAROLINA 27602

February 3, 1984

Dear Mr. Exum:

Thank you for your letter to the editor, but we cannot use it.

During an election time especially, we cannot permit letters not pegged to the news of a campaign to be run. We do not accept generalized endorsement or opposition letters.

Further, hyperbole -- such as your contention that the SBI checked out every service station in the state -- is inappropriate in this context.

Sincerely,

Associate Editor

a

FG/kt

Mr. Joe Exum
2106 Dallas Drive
Kinston, NC 28501

So edit the letter to read "almost every service station." Nobody's perfect! If truth should become a part of your editorial policy in the future, perhaps you can use it then.

In the meantime, can you believe the ugly things they're saying about Jimmy Green? Anyway, it's good to know you guys are keeping vigil over first amendment rights! Right!?

P.S. Glad to see Kathy finally got her paper route. You could be next in line.

*Letter from The News and Observer*

JESSE HELMS
NORTH CAROLINA

## United States Senate

WASHINGTON, DC 20510–3301

June 2, 1995

The Honorable Joe Exum
P. O. Box 475
Snow Hill, N.C. 28580

My dear Joe:

My late friend Chub Seawell used to
talk a lot about people whom he described
as having uncommon common sense.  I've always
placed you in that category--and your May 17
letter validates this characterization all
over again.

I'm making a copy of your letter to
deposit in my desk on the Senate Floor.  I
have a hunch that there'll be many times
when I can quote from it.

Forgive me, but I expecially enjoyed No.
5.

Sursum corda!

JESSE HELMS:fj

*Letter from the late Senator Jesse Helms*

and unlock it, I've
read alot in books
about them and know
alot. I know to keep it
and what to do to make
money. I hope you can
help me. Here's my address:

and again I say
I hope you can help
me!

Signed,

Signed,
Sarah

Snow Hill, North Carolina 28580 • P. O. Box 475 • Highway 258 South • 919-747-2911

January 7, 1982

Miss Sarah

Syracuse, N.Y. 13219

Dear Sarah,

We have read your letter with great interest and sincerely hope we can help.

You will be glad to know my brother and I have a boy and girl just about your age. In fact, Ann wanted a horse for Christmas also. However, there was no place for her to keep the horse and she decided to wait another year.

The best time to approach Mommas is a difficult question. It is our opinion mealtime is probably not a good time to ask about the horse. Perhaps bedtime is the best time to talk to your mom. We believe the best way to ask is to tell your mom exactly what you have in mind. Tell her exactly what you told us: how much you know about horses, and how you plan to help with expenses. Taking care of an animal, especially a horse, requires a lot of love, not to mention money. One thing about Mommas, they understand a lot more than we know!

We hope you won't mind, but we are sending copies of your letter to the editors of WESTERN HORSEMAN magazine and the SYRACUSE POST-STANDARD. They are _real_ experts. Call us no charge 1-800-334-8350 to let us know what happens. We will wait for your call.

Very truly yours,

HAPPY JACK, INC.

Joe Exum
Vice-President

_ask for Happy Jack . . your dog would_

*Correspondence between Sarah from Syracuse, NY and Joe Exum, Sr.*

CPSIA information can be obtained
at www.ICGtesting.com
Printed in the USA
LVHW080151200922
728811LV00015B/880